AT THE LIGHTING OF THE LAMPS

HYMNS OF THE ANCIENT CHURCH

MOREHOUSE PUBLISHING

Published in Great Britain by SLG Press,
Convent of the Incarnation

Published in America by
Morehouse Publishing
P.O. Box 1321
Harrisburg, PA 17105

Library of Congress Cataloging-in-Publication Data

At the lighting of the lamps : hymns of the ancient church / [compiled
and translated by] John Anthony McGuckin.
     p. cm.
   English, with Greek or Latin on facing pages.
   Originally published: Oxford, England : SLG Press, 1995.
   Includes bibliographical references.
   ISBN 0-8192-1717-4 (pbk.)
   1. Hymns, Greek—Translations into English. 2. Hymns, Latin—
Translations into English. 3. Hymns, Greek—Texts. 4. Hymns,
Latin—Texts.   I. McGuckin, John Anthony.
BV467.A8   1997
264'.011023—dc21
                                       97-37690
                                          CIP

Printed in the United States of America

Elenae   Uxori   Dilectae

CONTENTS

Introduction   ix

TRANSLATIONS OF THE HYMNS

1. *Hymn to the Creative Word* (John 1:1ff)   2-5
2. *Hymn of the Servant* (Phil. 2:5-11)   6-7
3. *Hymn to the Cosmic Lord* (Col. 1:13-20)   8-9
4. *Hymn to Christ* (1 Tim. 3:16)   10-11
5. *Hymn of Moses and the Lamb* (Rev. 15:3-4)   12-13
6. Clement of Alexandria, *Hymn to Christ the Shepherd*   14-17
7. *Jesus Christ, The Gladdening Light*   18-19
8. *The Cherubic Hymn*   20-21
9. *Eucharistic Hymn*   22-23
10. *Akathist to the Mother of God*   24-27
11. St Gregory Nazianzen, *Hymn of Thanksgiving*   28-31
12. St Ambrose, *A Hymn at Dawn*   32-35
13. St Ambrose, *Christ, Splendour of the Father's Glory* 36-37
14. Pseudo Ambrose, *Blessed Light*   38-39
15. Synesios of Cyrene, *The Eighth Hymn*   40-45
16. Merobaudes, *A Song of Christ*   46-49
17. Merobaudes, *A Paschal Hymn*   50-53
18. Prudentius, *A Hymn Before Eating*   54-57
19. Prudentius, *Hymn at the Lighting of the Lamps*   58-61
20. *A Grace before Eating*   62-63
21. *A Hymn at Eventide*   64-65
22. *An Evening Hymn*   66-67

23. *A Moral Palindrome*   68-69

24. St Romanos The Singer, *A Christmas Hymn*   70-73

25. St John of Damascus, *Hymn on the Resurrection*   74-75

26. St John of Damascus, *Hymn to the Virgin*   76-77

27. St John of Damascus, *Hymn to the Life-Giving Cross*   78-79

28. St John of Damascus,
        Hymn on the Presentation of the Lord   80-81

29. Sedulius, *A Paschal Song*   82-83

30. St Andrew of Jerusalem,
        Verses on the Birth of Christ   84-87

31. Pseudo Synesios, *The Prayer of the Scribe*   88-89

INTRODUCTION

The Christian Gospel began with a hymn, when angels in a lambent sky sang: 'Glory to God in the highest heaven, and peace to men on earth'. The last words of Jesus on the cross were also a hymn, for in his suffering he recited words familiar to him from childhood, the verses of Psalm 22. In the form of the Psalter, hymns have been at the centre of Jewish worship, and then of Christian, from the time of their composition in the first millenium BC. From earliest times at moments of spiritual joy or crisis Christians have turned instinctively to the medium of the canticle to express their deepest prayers and longings to the Lord.

Hymns are a central scriptural reality, and as such they are a major factor in shaping theological expression in the context of worship. They are the primary way in which Israel and the Church have developed a theological tradition. While the psalms are the greatest and most obvious collection of cultic hymns, there are many other hymnal forms in the Old Testament: for example, Exodus 15:1ff; Judges 5:3-5; Job 5:9-16, 12:13-25; Isaiah 42:10-12, 44:23, 52:9-10; Sir. 39:14-35 and 42:15-43:33. Some of these the Christian tradition designated as 'The Odes'.

The Old Testament hymn is similar in many respects to other ancient Near Eastern cultic songs (see ANET 365-368; 370-375; 383; 385-386; 387-389). But from the first the hymns of Israel stood out as dedicated to the celebration of the supreme Lord God and his providential care of his elect nation. Thus they are distinctive in having a strongly soteriological aspect, a character which Christianity retained and developed in its own tradition.

As well as the Psalms and Odes, hymns have been used in Christian liturgy from the earliest days of the Church (see Acts 16:25; Eph. 5:19). These were obviously of the Church's own composition, so a most important indicator of how it defined its own identity in the worship of its Risen Lord by describing the wonders that Christ had achieved in them and for them. This aspect of Christian hymns being a vivid encapsulation of the spirit and doctrine of the ancient community is something that endured for centuries, and can be said to apply even today in contemporary worship.

A characteristic aspect of the New Testament and the Patristic hymns was their strong christological focus. Pliny the Younger, when serving in Asia Minor, had to make an investigation into the Christians of his province, and described the Christian practice of worship in a very early letter. The one thing that had most clearly impressed him as an outsider was the practice of singing a hymn celebrating the divinity of Jesus: 'They meet and sing a hymn to Christ as if to a god' (*Christo quasi deo*).

Several of the most ancient Christian hymns have survived in the text of the New Testament itself, some quite obvious to the reader even today. They are quoted *in situ* by the biblical writer to illustrate a point or remind his hearers of an attitude, just as today to give an extra force to our words we would cite or allude to a well-known poem to an audience which we expected would recognize the allusion. In other cases the original hymn has been heavily reworked by the biblical writer, melded into the new text he is composing, and subsumed to the theological point he wishes to make for himself. Such hymns are more difficult to discern, but there is general agreement among biblical exegetes not only that such hymns exist, but also in some cases even as to the form that they might originally have had.

There are many other theorists who claim to recognize New Testament hymns where others see only a seamless text. The First Letter of Peter has been a favourite battleground in this regard. In the scriptural section of the present translations I have mainly kept to the straight and narrow, presenting some of the commonly agreed hymnic units. In them all the strong cosmic christology is remarkably evident, and in some instances the antiquity of the date is astounding. One such famous example is the hymn in Philippians 2:5-11. Given that St Paul is here quoting an element which he expects the Philippian church will generally recognize, then the poem must already be well established in their common worship. As Paul is himself writing *circa* AD 56, the hymn has to be earlier, thus easily within two decades of the death of Jesus. This means that, along with archetypal credal confessions (of the type represented by the hymn in 1 Tim. 3:16 in this collection), the christological hymn is one of the earliest forms of articulated Christian theology, predating even its genres of epistle or gospel.

Many of the New Testament hymns are so well known that it would be presumptuous to include them in this volume. They have for centuries been used as separate elements in the Church's formal worship at the liturgies of evening and morning prayers, for example, in both the Eastern and Western Church. This would apply to such major texts as The Magnificat (Luke 1:46ff); The Benedictus (Luke 2:29-32); or The Marriage Song of The Lamb (Rev. 19:1ff). While these major hymns are not represented (although the Nunc Dimittis sneaks in with John Damascene), five others have been chosen to remind readers of the extent and richness of this hymnal tradition in the New Testament itself. All five hymns are revealing in the shape and form of the christology they propound: a cosmic vision of redemption which goes on to inspire the greatest writers among the Greek and Latin Fathers.

The first of these is the hymn which opens the Fourth Gospel. This has been somewhat 'restored' to reach the state in which it now is offered. The hymnal rhythm of the Johannine Prologue is obvious, yet there has been much dispute as to the origin of the text, its original intent, and its relationship to the rest of the Gospel. The rhythm of the Logos hymn is quite clearly disrupted at several junctures by material about John the Baptist. These 'intrusions' are themselves less rhythmical in style and are bent on making a particular apologetic point, while the rest of the text is clearly celebrating the cosmic redemption brought by the Logos. It is a relatively easy matter to excise the John Baptist verses so that the remaining material slides back together seamlessly, with a majestic rhythmic culmination. This, I would suggest, is the original version which underwent editorial handling in the process of the several drafts that comprised the making of the Fourth Gospel. Its general structure and purpose thus mirrors and advances on Sirach 24, a text on which it is closely based. If the reader is not convinced by such textual presuppositions it matters little, for it is never misspent time to dwell on the masterly writing that comprises the Gospel of John. Even if the present rendition throws only a little new light on the text that now stands as our canonical version, it will not have been a wholly wasted exercise.

The patristic hymns included here range from simple liturgical songs, such as the *Phos Hilaron*, the chaste and charming hymn for the time of lamplighting, to some highly crafted works of literature, such as those pieces from the pens of skilled rhetors of the like of Gregory Nazianzen, Merobaudes, Prudentius, or Synesios of Cyrene. Some of the latter are so consciously crafted, and have such a personal and immediate sense, that they most nearly approach religious poetry in the modern understanding. Gregory's works, written in retirement, are often in this mode, but even so careful a craftsman as Synesios can still produce hymns of the highest intellectual order which can yet bear the strain, of communal recitation. Sedulius's exquisite 'Paschal Song' is distinctive in that it is not addressed to God at all, rather to his friend Tado, archbishop of Milan. It reflects the freshness of Easter day in a different way to the Greek and Latin doxologies, evoking a more personal inner landscape where the murmuring bees and Easter flowers turn his mind and heart to absent friends as he imagines them celebrating the Easter liturgies.

It is hardly an innovative work to present again many of these pieces, although I have chosen with an eye to some fresh things, and it is doubtless true that each generation has its own need to reappropriate its classics. Many of the Victorian and Edwardian writers, such as J. H. Newman, J. M. Neale, John Brownlie, or R. M. Pope, who attempted ancient hymnal translations, were stalwarts who set them into English verse form. I am not so stalwart. Although their efforts often command respect, and Pope's Prudentius is one such case, in the main the effort at compromise between exact translation and the demands of English rhyming schemes leaves the outcome stranded on the shores of versification, a distinctly different thing from poetry.

Today, with our much greater readiness to accept free verse as normal than ever previous generations had, there seems little point in preferring rhyming verse to an attempt at graceful and poetic English that tries to catch the spirit of the original, yet with a firm hand on textual authenticity. Such has been the design of the present translations. If, as seems to be the case, the famous hymnal translation of Pseudo-Synesios', 'Lord Jesus think on me, and purge away my sin', is actually the rendition of the Pseudo-Synesios text included at the end of this volume, then one can only marvel at how far poetic licence has in the past been felt to extend.

I would have liked to present all the literature complete and unexpurgated, but it has to be confessed that the more literate of the ancients had a propensity to dwell on details and advance more digressions than most of us have the patience to follow in these busy days. It is also generally the case that the more elaborated the hymnal form is in the hands of the rhetors, the less likely it was ever to have been used in the real worship of the Church. There are exceptions to this, as in the great Akathist Hymn, which is still used in Eastern ritual, or the long hymns of Romanos which had, and still do have, a place in the unfolding of the Offices of Hours in the East. Nevertheless, it is true about Prudentius, and Sedulius. From early centuries the Roman church recognized the great beauty and worth of the former's poetry, and reused it in the breviary with extensive cuts.

I have been emboldened by this bad example, and so have made cuts and edited the material, but generally only in the longer hymns such as the Akathist, or with parts of Romanos, John Damascene, Prudentius, and Sedulius. Where I have done this, it is made clear in the notes accompanying the texts at the back of this volume. Otherwise I have given the text of the whole work. The annotations also offer a very brief set of comments on relevant historical and theological aspects of the texts. Each hymn demands a far fuller commentary to do justice to it, but I have tried in a few strokes to suggest something of the context and allusions that might assist a reader's appreciation of a given piece.

To repair the dishonour inflicted on these great men by the presumption of forcing them into English, I have presented the original Greek and Latin forms in parallel to the translations. This allows the style and flow of the originals to become evident. As they were all designed for open recitation, it will be a revealing and pleasant exercise to read them out loud, at least in the Latin forms which follow (by and large) the phonetic rules one would expect. For those who have no Greek it is only a matter of a few days' practice to acquire the phonetic skills that would allow oral declamation of the Eastern pieces. To assist this, as well as to offer some solace to those who were taught New Testament Greek through the Erasmian pronunciation system, there is a pronunciation guide to Greek given below. This follows Byzantine phonetic practice, very similar to modern Greek. It is arguably the correct way to pronounce the New Testament texts (there is a recorded conversation between Tiberius and Caesar Augustus which only makes sense if one presumes an approximation to Byzantine phonetics), but it is undoubtedly the correct way to pronounce the Greek patristic texts.

Offering the original forms should also allow readers with linguistic skills to practise their own translations. Since this might also invite criticisms of my renderings, let me add that I have tried only to depart from a close rendition when poetic licence seized me. On that basis I think I can avoid most complaints.

The collection of hymns here is a personal selection, but I feel that it justly represents the spirit of the ancient Church, and what is more, a spirit imbued with the deepest sense of prayerful worship of the Lord of Glory. Such texts are not only graceful in their literary merit, they also breathe the gracefulness of prayer upon those who read or sing them. And I trust that if anyone is moved to apply them for the purpose for which they were originally created, they might be kind enough, at the time of the lighting of the lamps of evening, or the dawning of a new day, those times when Christians first used their hymns, to remember the translator on occasion.

JOHN McGUCKIN
The University of Leeds
Feast of St Eirene the Great Martyr, 1995

PRONUNCIATION GUIDE TO BYZANTINE GREEK

The accents suggest where the emphasis is to be placed. An acute accent signifies a slight raising of the tone over that vowel while placing the stress there. A grave accent suggests a slight lowering of the tone while stressing the point. A circumflex accent suggests a very slight lingering or lengthening of the vowel as a stress. Hard and soft breathings have, to all intents and purposes, disappeared in Byzantine Greek. Ignore all marks ' or ' at the opening vowel of words. Everything is rendered into a soft breathing (unaspirated).

The vowels and consonants have the following values:

α	a as in pat	β	v as in velvet
γ	g as in got	δ	d as in depth
ε	e as in egg	ζ	dz as in adze
η	ee as in peek	θ	th as in eighth
ι	ee as in peek	κ	k as in cat
λ	l as in lap	μ	m as in mum
ν	n as in nun	ξ	xs as in ox
ο	o as in pot	π	p as in pot
ρ	rh as in rhododendron	ς σ	s as in salt
τ	t as in tap	υ	ee as in peek
φ	as in film	χ	aspirated h pronounced roughly
ψ	ps as in apse	ω	o as in pot

Adjacent letters normally sound separately; vowel combinations (dipthongs) have the following values:

ει; οι; υι all sound *ee* as in peek.
ευ sounds *ef.* αυ sounds *af.* (εὐχάριστος sounds *efhareestos*).
αι sounds *e* as in pet. ου sounds *oo* as in spook.
When two γγ letters occur they are sounded *ng* as in rung.
If γκ occurs it is sounded *nk* as in tank.

Thus, taking Hymn 9 as an example, the first three lines would sound:

> Too deepnoo soo too meestikoo
> seemeron eeay theoo
> keenonon meh paralaveh.

The first three lines of hymn 26 would sound:

> Teen pangkosmion doxan
> teen ex anthropon spareesan
> keh ton despoteen tekoosan.

And the Palindrome of Hymn 23 would sound:

> Neepson anomeemata mee monan opseen.

THE POEMS

1. ΚΑΤΑ ΙΩΑΝΝΗΝ

Ἐν ἀρχῇ ἦν ὁ λόγος,
καὶ ὁ λόγος ἦν πρὸς τὸν θεόν,
καὶ θεὸς ἦν ὁ λόγος.
οὗτος ἦν ἐν ἀρχῇ πρὸς τὸν θεόν.

πάντα δι᾽ αὐτοῦ εγένετο,
καὶ χωρὶς αὐτοῦ ἐγένετο οὐδὲ ἕν.
ὃ γέγονεν ἐν αὐτῷ ζωὴ ἦν,
καὶ ἡ ζωὴ ἦν τὸ φῶς τῶν ἀνθρώπων·
καὶ τὸ φῶς ἐν τῇ σκοτίᾳ φαίνει,
καὶ ἡ σκοτία αὐτὸ οὐ κατέλαβεν.

Ἦν τὸ φῶς τὸ ἀληθινόν,
ὃ φωτίζει πάντα ἄνθρωπον,
ἐρχόμενον εἰς τὸν κόσμον.
ἐν τῷ κόσμῳ ἦν,
καὶ ὁ κόσμος δι᾽ αὐτοῦ ἐγένετο,
καὶ ὁ κόσμος αὐτὸν οὐκ ἔγνω.
εἰς τὰ ἴδια ἦλθεν,
καὶ οἱ ἴδιοι αὐτὸν οὐ παρέλαβον.
ὅσοι δὲ ἔλαβον αὐτόν
ἔδωκεν αὐτοῖς ἐξουσίαν τέκνα θεοῦ γενέσθαι,

τοῖς πιστεύουσιν εἰς τὸ ὄνομα αὐτοῦ,
οἳ οὐκ ἐξ αἱμάτων
οὐδὲ ἐκ θελήματος σαρκὸς
οὐδὲ ἐκ θελήματος ἀνδρὸς
ἀλλ᾽ ἐκ θεοῦ ἐγεννήθησαν.

Hymn to the Creative Word

In the beginning was the Word
and the Word was with God
and the Word was God
who was with God in the beginning.
All things came through him
and apart from him came nothing.
What came in him was Life
the life that was the light of men,
which light is shining in the darkness
and the darkness cannot grasp it.
The Word was the True Light
which illumines every man
and came into the world.
He was in the world
for the world had come through him
yet the world did not know him.
He came to his own
and his own did not receive him
but as many as received him
he gave the stature of being children of God.
These were the ones who believed in his name;
For them it was not blood,
or the stir of the flesh,
not the mere choice of man
that gave them birth,
for they were born of God.

Καὶ ὁ λόγος σὰρξ ἐγένετο
καὶ ἐσκήνωσεν ἐν ἡμῖν,
καὶ ἐθεασάμεθα τὴν δόξαν αὐτοῦ,
δόξαν ὡς μονογενοῦς παρὰ πατρός,
πλήρης χάριτος καὶ ἀληθείας.

ὅτι ἐκ τοῦ πληρώματος αὐτοῦ ἡμεῖς πάντες ἐλάβομεν
καὶ χάριν ἀντὶ χάριτος·
ὅτι ὁ νόμος διὰ Μωυσέως ἐδόθη,
ἡ χάρις καὶ ἡ ἀλήθεια δὶ Ἰησοῦ Χριστοῦ ἐγένετο.

Θεὸν οὐδεὶς ἑώρακεν πώποτε·
μονογενὴς θεὸς
ὁ ὢν εἰς τὸν κόλπον τοῦ πατρὸς
ἐκεῖνος ἐξηγήσατο.

And the Word became flesh
and sojourned in our midst
and we gazed upon his glory
the glory of the Sole-Begotten of the Father,
full of grace and truth.
From his fullness we have all received
grace on grace abundant,
for the Law was given through Moses
but grace and truth came through Jesus Christ.
No man has ever looked on God.
Only that Sole-Begotten God
in the very bosom of the Father.
Only he has made him known.

Gospel of St John, 1st century
John 1:1-5, 9-14, 16-18

2

ΠΡΟΣ ΦΙΛΙΠΠΗΣΙΟΤΣ

Τοῦτο φρονεῖτε ἐν ὑμῖν
ὃ καὶ ἐν Χριστῷ Ἰησοῦ,
ὃς ἐν μορφῇ θεοῦ ὑπάρχων
οὐχ ἁρπαγμὸν ἡγήσατο
τὸ εἶναι ἴσα θεῷ,

ἀλλὰ ἑαυτὸν εκένωσεν
μορφὴν δούλου λαβών,
ἐν ὁμοιώματι ἀνθρώπων γενόμενος·

καὶ σχήματι εὑρεθεὶς ὡς ἄνθρωπος
ἐταπείνωσεν ἑαυτὸν
γενόμενος ὑπήκοος μέχρι θανάτου,
θανάτου δὲ σταυροῦ.

διὸ καὶ ὁ θεὸς αὐτὸν ὑπερύψωσεν
καὶ ἐχαρίσατο αὐτῷ τὸ ὄνομα τὸ ὑπὲρ πᾶν ὄνομα,
ἵνα ἐν τῷ ὀνόματι Ἰησοῦ πᾶν γόνυ κάμψῃ
ἐπουρανίων καὶ ἐπιγείων καὶ καταχθονίων
καὶ πᾶσα γλῶσσα ἐξομολογήσηται
ὅτι κύριος Ἰησοῦς Χριστὸς
εἰς δόξαν θεοῦ πατρός.

Hymn of the Servant

Have this conception among you
which was Christ Jesus' own,
for though he was in the form of God
he did not arrogate to himself
an equal standing with the Deity.

He forsook himself
to assume the form of a slave
and came in the likeness of men.

He was found in fashion as a man
and humbled himself
becoming obedient to the point of death;
a death by crucifixion.

For this, God exalted him most highly
and graced him with the name above all names,
so at the name of Jesus every knee shall bend,
all creatures of the Heavens, Earth, and Shades,
and every tongue shall confess
that Jesus Christ is Lord,
to the glory of God the Father.

Letter of Paul to the Philippians
1st century
Phil. 2:5-11

3. ΠΡΟΣ ΚΟΛΟΣΣΑΕΙΣ

ὅς ἐστιν εἰκὼν τοῦ θεοῦ τοῦ ἀοράτου,
πρωτότοκος πάσης κτίσεως,
ὅτι ἐν αὐτῷ ἐκτίσθη τὰ πάντα
ἐν τοῖς οὐρανοῖς καὶ ἐπὶ τῆς γῆς,
τὰ ὁρατὰ καὶ τὰ ἀόρατα,
εἴτε θρόνοι εἴτε κυριότητες
εἴτε ἀρχαὶ εἴτε ἐξουσίαι·

τὰ πάντα δι᾽ αὐτοῦ
καὶ εἰς αὐτὸν ἔκτισται,
καὶ αὐτός ἐστιν πρὸ πάντων
καὶ τὰ πάντα ἐν αὐτῷ συνέστηκεν.

καὶ αὐτός ἐστιν ἡ κεφαλὴ τοῦ σώματος,
        τῆς ἐκκλησίας·
ὅς ἐστιν ἀρχή,
πρωτότοκος ἐκ τῶν νεκρῶν,
ἵνα γένηται ἐν πᾶσιν αὐτος πρωτεύων,

ὅτι ἐν αὐτῷ εὐδόκησεν
        πᾶν τὸ πλήρωμα κατοικῆσαι
καὶ δι᾽ αὐτοῦ ἀποκαταλλάξαι
        τὰ πάντα εἰς αὐτόν,
εἰρηνοποιήσας διὰ τοῦ αἵματος
        τοῦ σταυροῦ αὐτοῦ,
εἴτε τὰ ἐπὶ τῆς γῆς
        εἴτε τὰ ἐν τοῖς οὐρανοῖς.

3

Hymn to the Cosmic Lord

He is the Icon of the Unseen God
The First-Born of all creation
for in Him were made all that is
in the Heavens and on the Earth,
all that is unseen, and seen;
the Thrones, Dominions,
Principalities and Powers.

All things were made through Him,
and for His sake.
He exists before them all
and all find stable unity in him.

He is the Head of the Body
       which is the Church.
He is the Beginning,
the First-Born from the dead,
and, through that, first in every way.

In Him the whole Pleroma pleased to dwell
to bring back to Itself all things through Him,
on the Earth, or in the Heavens,
granting peace through the blood of His cross.

Letter to the Colossians
1st century
Col. 1:15-20

4

ΠΡΟΣ ΤΙΜΟΘΕΟΝ Α

Καὶ ὁμολογουμένως μέγα ἐστὶν
τὸ τῆς εὐσεβείας μυστήριον·

Ὃς ἐφανερώθη ἐν σαρκί,
ἐδικαιώθη ἐν πνεύματι,
ὤφθη ἀγγέλοις,
ἐκηρύχθη ἐν ἔθνεσιν,
ἐπιστεύθη ἐν κόσμῳ,
ἀνελήμφθη ἐν δόξῃ.

4

Hymn to Christ

How truly great
is the mystery of our religion

He was revealed in the flesh,
vindicated in the spirit,
seen by the angels,
proclaimed among the nations,
believed on in the world,
taken up in glory.

Letter of Paul to Timothy
1st century
1 Tim. 3:16

5

ΑΠΟΚΑΛΥΨΙΣ ΙΩΑΝΝΟΥ

Μεγάλα καὶ θαυμαστὰ τὰ ἔργα σου,
Κύριε ὁ Θεὸς ὁ Παντοκράτωρ·
δίκαια καὶ ἀληθιναὶ αἱ ὁδοί σου,
ὁ βασιλεὺς τῶν αἰώνων.

Τίς οὐ μὴ φοβηθῇ, Κύριε,
καὶ δοξάσει τὸ ὄνομά σου ;
ὅτι μόνος ὅσιος,
ὅτι πάντα τὰ ἔθνη ἥξουσιν
καὶ προσκυνήσουσιν ἐνώπιόν σου,
ὅτι τὰ δικαιώματά σου ἐφανερώθησαν.

5

Hymn of Moses and the Lamb

Great and wonderful are your works
O Lord God, Master of All,
Your ways are righteous and true,
O King of The Aeons.

Lord, who shall not tremble before you,
or give glory to your name?
For you alone are The Holy One
and all the nations shall draw near,
shall bow down in your presence,
since your righteous judgements have been revealed.

The Book of Revelation
1st century
Rev. 15:3-4

6.   ΧΡΙΣΤΟΣ Ο ΠΟΙΜΗΝ

Στόμιον πώλων ἀδαμῶν,
πτερὸν ὀρνίθιων ἀπλανῶν,
οἴαξ νηῶν ἀτρεκής,
ποιμὴν ἀρνῶν βασιλικῶν·
τοὺς σοὺς ἀφελεῖς παῖδας ἄγειρον
αἰνεῖν ἀγίως,
ὑμνεῖν ἀδόλως
ἀκάκοις στόμασιν
παίδων ἡγήτορα Χριστόν.
Βασιλεῦ ἀγίων,
λόγε πανδαμάτωρ
πατρὸς ὑψίστου,
σοφίας πρύτανι,
στήριγμα πόνων
αἰωνοχαρές,
βροτέας γενεᾶς
σῶτερ Ἰησοῦ,
ποιμήν, ἀροτήρ,
οἴαξ, στόμιον,
πτερὸν οὐράνιον
παναγοῦς ποίμνης,
ἀλιεῦ μερόπων
τῶν σωζομένων,
πελάγους κακίας
ἰχθῦς ἀγνοὺς
κύματος ἐχθροῦ
γλυκερᾷ ζωῇ δελεάζων.
Ἡγοῦ, προβάτων
λογικῶν ποιμήν,
ἄγιε, ἡγοῦ,
βασιλεῦ παίδων ἀνεπάφων.

14

6

Hymn to Christ the Shepherd

Bridle for wild horses,
Wing of birds unerring,
Dead-set helm for ships,
Shepherd of royal lambs,

Gather your simple children
To praise holily,
To hymn guilelessly
With innocent mouths,
Christ the Guide of children.

Lord of saints,
All-subduing Word of the Most High Father,
Master of Wisdom,
Strong support of griefs,
Rejoicing in eternity:
Jesus, Saviour of the Mortal race,
Shepherd, Ploughman, Helm, and Bridle,
Heavenly Wing over the all-holy flock,
Fisher of men who have been saved,
Catching pure fish with the sweet bait of life,
from a sea of evil and the enemy's waves.
Shepherd of rational sheep,
Guide us, Holy King,
As unspoilt children,
In the footsteps of Christ.

Ἴχνια Χριστοῦ, ὁδὸς οὐρανία,
λόγος ἀέναος,
αἰὼν ἄπλετος,
φῶς ἀίδιον,
ἐλέους πηγή,
ῥεκτὴρ ἀρετῆς,
σεμνὴ βιοτὴ
θεὸν ὑμνούντων,
Χριστὲ Ἰησοῦ,
γάλα οὐράνιον
μαστῶν γλυκερῶν
νύμφης χαρίτων,
σοφίας τῆς σῆς,
ἐκθλιβόντων,
τοὺς σοὺς ἀφελεῖς
παῖδας ἄγειρον,
αἰνεῖν ἁγίως,
ὑμνεῖν ἀδόλως
ἀκάκοις στόμασιν
παίδων ἡγητόρα Χριστόν.
Οἱ νηπίαχοι
ἀταλοῖς στόμασιν
ἀτιταλλόμενοι
θηλῆς λογικῆς,
πνεύματι δροσερῷ
ἐμπιπλάμενοι
αἴνους ἀφελεῖς,
ὕμνους ἀτρεκεῖς
βασιλεῖ Χριστῷ
μισθοὺς ὁσίους
ζωῆς διδαχῆς
μέλπωμεν ὁμοῦ·
χορὸς εἰρήνης,
οἱ χριστόγονοι,
λαὸς σώφρων,
ψάλλωμεν ὁμοῦ
θεὸν εἰρήνης.

Heavenly Way,
Ever-flowing Word,
Immeasurable Aeon,
Eternal Light,
Fount of Mercy,
Adept in Virtue.
How noble is the life
Of those who sing to God.
Christ Jesus, Heavenly Milk
Of those sweet breasts
Of the graces of the Bride,
Pressed from your wisdom.

Gather your simple children,
To praise holily,
To hymn guilelessly,
With innocent mouths,
Christ the Guide of children;

Little children,
So tender their gums,
Feeding to the full
With spiritual dew
From the nipple of your Wisdom.

Together let us raise a merry sound
To Christ the King,
Of simple praises, and true hymns,
Rewards of the Doctrine of Life.
Let us sing together,
All you who are Christ-begotten,
A Sober People,
A Chorus of peace,
To the God of Peace.

Clement of Alexandria
Late 2nd century

7

ΥΜΝΟΣ ΕΠΙΛΥΧΝΙΟΣ

Φῶς ἱλαρὸν ἁγίας δόξης,
ἀθανάτου πατρὸς οὐρανίου,
ἁγίου, μάκαρος,
Ἰησοῦ Χριστέ,
ἐλθόντες ἐπὶ τὴν ἡλίου δύσιν,
ἰδόντες φῶς ἑσπερινὸν
ὑμνοῦμεν πατέρα, υἱὸν
καὶ ἅγιον πνεῦμα θεόν.
Ἄξιος εἶ ἐν πᾶσι καιροῖς
ὑμνεῖσθαι φωναῖς αἰσίαις,
Υἱὲ Θεοῦ, ζωὴν ὁ διδούς·
διὸ κόσμος σε δοξάζει.

Jesus Christ, the Gladdening Light

Jesus Christ,
the Gladdening Light
of the deathless Father's
holy glory;
the heavenly,
holy, blessed one.

As the sun reclines
we see the light of evening
and sing our hymn to God,
The Father, Son, and Holy Spirit.

Worthy are you, O Son of God,
through each and every moment,
that joyful songs should hymn you.

You are the giver of our life,
and so the world gives glory.

The Greek Liturgy of the Hours
Anonymous
circa 3rd century

8

Η ΜΕΓΑΛΗ ΕΙΣΟΔΟΣ

Οἱ τὰ Χερουβεὶμ
μυστικῶς εἰκονίζοντες
καὶ τῇ ζωοποιῷ Τριάδι
τὸν τρισάγιον ὕμνον προσᾴδοντες,
πᾶσαν τὴν βιοτικὴν ἀποθώμεθα μέριμναν·
ὡς τὸν βασιλέα τῶν ὅλων ὑποδεξόμενοι
ταῖς ἀγγελικαῖς ἀοράτως δορφορούμενον τάξεσιν.
Ἀλληλούια. Ἀλληλούια. Ἀλληλούια.

The Cherubic Hymn

We, the mystical symbols,
Of the Cherubim,
Also offer the thrice holy hymn
to the Trinity that gives all life.

Let us set aside all earth-bound care
To receive the King of All,
Escorted round
By unseen ranks of angels.
Alleluia, Alleluia, Alleluia.

Liturgy of St John Chrysostom
circa 5th century

9

ΤΟΥ ΔΕΙΠΝΟΥ ΣΟΥ

Τοῦ δείπνου σου τοῦ μυστικοῦ,
σήμερον Υἱὲ Θεοῦ,
κοινωνόν με παράλαβε·
οὐ μὴ γὰρ τοῖς ἐχθροῖς σου τὸ μυστήριον εἴπω·
οὐ φίλημά σοι δώσω καθάπερ ὁ Ἰούδας·
ἀλλ᾽ ὡς ὁ ληστὴς ὁμολογῶ σοι·
Μνήσθητί μου Κύριε,
ἐν τῇ βασιλείᾳ σου.

9

Eucharistic Hymn

This day receive me
Son of God,
Communing at your mystic feast,
For I will not betray
Your Mystery to your foes;
Will never give a kiss
Like that which Judas gave,
But like the thief
I shall confess to you:
In your royal Kingdom, Lord,
Be mindful then of me.

Liturgy of St John Chrysostom
circa 5th century

10

ΑΚΑΘΙΣΤΟΣ ΥΜΝΟΣ

Τῇ ὑπερμάχῳ στρατηγῷ τὰ νικητήρια,
ὡς λυτρωθεῖσα τῶν δεινῶν, εὐχαριστήρια
ἀναγράφω σοι ἡ πόλις σου, Θεοτόκε·
ἀλλ᾿ ὡς ἔχουσα τὸ κράτος ἀπροσμάχητον
ἐκ παντοίων με κινδύνων ἐλευθέρωσον,
ἵνα κράζω σοι· χαῖρε, νύμφη ἀνύμφευτε.

Ἄγγελος πρωτοστάτης
οὐρανόθεν ἐπέμφθη
εἰπεῖν τῇ θεοτόκῳ τὸ χαῖρε·
καὶ σὺν τῇ ἀσωμάτῳ φωνῇ
σωματούμενόν σε θεωρῶν, κύριε,
ἐξίστατο καὶ ἵστατο,
κραυγάζων πρὸς αὐτὴν τοιαῦτα·

χαῖρε, δι᾿ ἧς ἡ χαρὰ ἐκλάμψει·
χαῖρε, δι᾿ ἧς ἡ ἀρὰ ἐκλείψει·
χαῖρε, τοῦ πεσόντος Ἀδὰμ ἡ ἀνάκλησις·
χαῖρε, τῶν δακρύων τῆς Εὔας ἡ λύτρωσις·
χαῖρε, ὕψος δυσανάβατον ἀνθρωπίνοις λογισμοῖς·
χαῖρε, βάθος δυσθεώρητον καὶ ἀγγέλων ὀφθαλμοῖς·
χαῖρε, ὅτι ὑπάρχεις βασιλέως καθέδρα·
χαῖρε, ὅτι βαστάζεις τὸν βαστάζοντα πάντα·

Akathist to the Mother of God

Our grateful thanks, O Mother of God,
I dedicate to you; our city's songs
Of Victory, to our unconquered heroine,
Who has redeemed us from such woes,
Whose power is irresistible,
Freeing us from all distress.
And thus I cry to you:

Hail Unwedded Bride.

An angel of the highest rank
Was sent from heaven above,
To say to the Virgin: All Hail.

And at this bodiless sound, O Lord,
He saw you come into the body's form.
He stood astounded and amazed,
And cried out to her saying:

Hail, through whom comes radiant joy.
Hail, through whom the curse has ceased.
Hail, lapsed Adam's restoration.
Hail, redemption of the tears of Eve.
Hail, unscalable height,
      beyond the mind of man.
Hail, great depth beyond all sight,
      even to angelic eyes.
Hail, royal throne.
Hail to you who bore,
      The One who bears all things.

χαῖρε, ἀστὴρ ἐμφαίνων τὸν ἥλιον·
χαῖρε, γαστὴρ ἐνθέου σαρκώσεως·
χαῖρε, δι᾽ ἧς νεουργεῖται ἡ κτίσις·
χαῖρε, δι᾽ ἧς βρεφουργεῖται ὁ κτίστης·
χαῖρε, νύμφη ἀνύμφευτε.

Hail, star that shows the sun.
Hail, womb of God's enfleshment.
Hail, through whom creation is renewed.
Hail, through whom the Creator
    Himself became a child.

All Hail, Unwedded Bride.

Byzantine (Romanos?) 6th century
Edited by Patriarch Sergius, 7th century

11

ΕΥΧΑΡΙΣΤΗΡΙΟΝ

Σοὶ χάρις, ὦ πάντων βασιλεῦ, πάντων δὲ ποιητά,
Σοὶ χάρις· ὃς τὰ νοητὰ λόγῳ,τά θ᾽ ὁρατὰ κελεύσει
Στῆσας τ᾽ οὐ πρὶν ἐόντα, καὶ ἐξ ἀφανοῦς κατέδειξας.
Σὸν θρόνον ἀμφιέπουσιν ἀκήρατοι ὑμνητῆρες,
Ἔνθεν μυριάδες, καὶ χιλιάδες πάλιν ἔνθεν,
Ἀγγελικῆς στρατιῆς πυρόεις χορὸς, ἄφθιτοι ἀρχὴν
Λαοὶ πρωτοτόκων, καὶ λαμπομένων χορὸς ἄστρων·
Πνεύματα θεσπεσίων ἀνδρῶν, ψυχαί τε δικαίων,
Πάντες ὁμηγερέες, καὶ σὸν θρόνον ἀμφιέποντες,
Γηθοσύνῃ τε, φόβῳ τε διηνεκὲς ἀείδουσι
Ὕμνον ἀνυμνείοντες ἀκήρατον, ἢ καὶ ἄπαυστον·
Σοὶ χάρις, ὦ πάντων βασιλεῦ, πάντων δὲ ποιητά.
Οὗτος ἀκήρατος ὕμνος ἐπ᾽ οὐρανίοιο χοροῖο.
Ναὶ λίτομαι καγὼ, Πάτερ ἄφθιτε, καὶ γόνυ κάμπτω
Ἡμετέρης κραδίης, Πάτερ ἄμβροτε, καὶ νόος ἔνδον
Πρηνής σου προπάροιθε· κάρη δέ μοι ἐς χθόνα νεύει
Λισσομένῳ· κεῖμαι δ᾽ ἱκέτης, καὶ δάκρυα χεύω
Οὐδὲ γὰρ ἄξιός εἰμι πρὸς οὐρανὸν ἀντία λεύσσειν
Ἀλλὰ σύ μ᾽ οἰκτείροις, ἐλέους Πάτερ, ἵλαος ἔσσο
Σῷ κινυρῷ θεράποντι· σάου δὲ με χεῖρα τανύσσας
Ἐξ ὀνύχων θανάτοιο, νοήματα πάντα καθήρας.
Μή μ᾽ ἀπογυμνώσῃς σοῦ Πνεύματος, ἀλλ᾽ ἔτι μᾶλλον
Χεῦε μένος καὶ θάρσος ἐνὶ στήθεσσιν ἐμοῖσιν·
Ὄφρα σε καὶ κραδίῃ, καὶ χείλεσι καλὸν ἀείσω.

Hymn Of Thanksgiving

All thanks to you, the King of All, and Maker of all things.
All thanks to you who by your Word,
      commanded spiritual and material forms,
And summoned into being what was not there before,
      from nothingness to bring them forth.
Those perfect singers of your praise
      stand gathered round your throne,
The myriad of angelic ranks, untold myriads yet again,
That fiery chorus all unmarred, since time has first begun,
The first-born nation, with a choir of radiant stars,
Those spirits of your righteous saints, the souls of all the just,
All are gathered in as one, to stand around your throne,
To make their hymn with ceaseless joy and awe.
They chant a song both endless and sublime:
'All thanks to you Most Mighty King and Maker of all things.'
A hymn indeed sublime, that issues from that heavenly choir.
And yet, I too shall make my prayer:
Immortal Father,
      Before you I shall bend the knee, to signify my heart;
Immortal Father,
      In your presence, I lay down my inmost mind prostrate.
I rest my brow upon the ground, to make my prayer to you.
And so I lie, a suppliant. My libation is my tears.
For how could I be worthy, to raise my eyes above?
Merciful Father, take pity on me.
Have mercy on your servant who thus implores your grace.
Stretch forth your hand, and cleanse my inmost thoughts,
And snatch me then from out the claws of death.
Of your Spirit never let me be bereft,
So pour your courage and your strength into this soul of mine,
That I may hymn you with my heart and voice.

Ὥσπερ ἐμῷ γενετῆρι, σῷ θεράποντι παρέστης,
Δὸς καὶ ἐμοὶ καθαρὸν βίοτον, καθαράν τε τελευτὴν,
Ἐλπωρήν τε τυχεῖν ἀγαθὴν, ἔλεόν τε, χάριν τε·
Πάντα δ᾿ ἀμαλδύνει, ὅσα ἥλιτον ἐκ νεότητος,
Ὡς ἀγαθὸς βασιλεύς· ὅτι σοὶ χάρις ἤματα πάντα,
Σοὶ χάρις ἤματα πάντα, καὶ εἰς αἰῶνας ἅπαντας.

I am your servant, but be a Father unto me,
And grant to me a blameless life, and grant a blameless end;
Grant me the hope to do the good, your mercy, and your grace,
That overlooks so many sins committed since my youth.
For you are my Good King indeed. To you all thanks are due.
All thanks are due to you. And unto every Age.

St Gregory Nazianzen
4th century

Carmen Aurorae

Aeterne rerum Conditor,
Noctem diemque qui regis,
Et temporum das tempora,
Ut alleves fastidium,
Praeco diei iam sonat,
Noctis profundae pervigil,
Nocturna lux viantibus,
A nocte noctem segregans.
Hoc excitatus lucifer,
Solvit polum caligine,
Hoc omnis erronum chorus,
Vias nocendi deserit.
Hoc nauta vires colligit,
Pontique mitescunt freta,
Hoc ipse petra Ecclesiae
Canente, culpam diluit.
Surgamus ergo strenue,
Gallus iacentes excitat,
Et somnolentos increpat,
Gallus negantes arguit.
Gallo canente, spes redit,
Aegris salus refunditur,
Mucro latronis conditur,
Lapsis fides revertitur.

A Hymn at Dawn

Eternal maker of all things,
Who rule both Day and Night,
And set the bounds on time itself
As respite for our frailty,

The herald of the day now sounds,
Watchful in the depth of night,
Telling travellers that first light has come,
Cutting off each night from night.

Thereby the Bringer of Light is roused,
And frees the skies of darkness.
At his cry, a throng of ills
Leaves off its evil ways.

At this the sailor gains new strength
And raging seas subside.
At his song, the church's very rock
Washed off his guilt in tears.

So let us rise with gladness.
The cockerel rouses those abed,
And scolds all tired laggards,
Shouting down who would resist.

At the cockerel's call, our hope renews,
The sick find health restored,
The robber's sword is sheathed,
The lapsed find faith again.

Jesu, labantes respice,
Et nos videndo corrige;
Si respicis, lapsus cadunt,
Fletuque culpa solvitur.
Tu, lux, refulge sensibus,
Mentisque somnum discute:
Te nostra vox primum sonet,
Et vota solvamus tibi.

Jesu, look on our frailty,
And by your gaze correct us.
If you look on, our faults shall fall away,
And guilt dissolve in tears.

Lord of light shine on our senses,
Scatter the phantoms of our mind.
Our voice shall hymn you first this day,
Offering up our prayers and vows.

St. Ambrose of Milan
4th century

13

Splendor Paternae Gloriae

Splendor paternae gloriae,
De luce lucem proferens,
Primordiis lucis novae
Diem dies illuminans.
Verusque sol illabere,
Micans nitore perpeti,
Jubarque Sancti Spiritus
Infunde nostris sensibus.
Votis vocemus et Patrem,
Patrem perennis gloriae,
Patrem potentis gratiae,
Culpam releget lubricam.
Informet actus strenuos,
Dentes retundat invidi,
Casus secundet asperos,
Donet gerendi gratiam.
Mentem gubernet et regat,
Casto fideli corpore,
Fides calore ferveat,
Fraudis venena nesciat.
Christusque nobis sit cibus,
Potusque noster sit fides;
Laeti bibamus sobriam
Ebrietatem Spiritus.
Laetus dies hic transeat;
Pudor sit ut diluculum,
Fides velut meridies,
Crepusculum mens nesciat.
Aurora cursus provehit,
Aurora totus prodeat
In Patre totus Filius
Et totus in Verbo Pater.

Christ, Splendour of the Father's Glory

Splendour of the Father's glory,
Bringing forth light from light.
Day illuminating daylight,
With new beginnings of new light;
True Sun come down,
Sparkling with unfailing gleams,
With the radiance of the Spirit,
Come fill us in our every sense.
And in prayer we call upon the Father,
That Father of unending glory,
Father of all-mastering grace.
Lord set aside our sinful guilt
And teach us eagerness of deed;
Restrain the biting teeth of foes,
Prosper us in times of grief,
Grant the grace to bring us through.
Guide and rule our inmost mind,
In a chaste and faithful heart.
May our faith grow hot again,
Far from poison's foul pretence.
Let Christ himself be all our food,
And faith our cup to drink;
Let us drain it deep in joy,
The sober drunkenness of Spirit.
Let this day be spent rejoicing.
Let shame be as the dimmest dawn,
And faith like midday sun;
Our minds ever ignorant of dusk.
The chariot of the rising sun sets forth,
The rising sun appears complete:
The Son complete within the Father,
The Father complete within the Word.

St. Ambrose of Milan
4th century

14

Lux Beata

O Lux, beata Trinitas
Et principalis Unitas,
Iam sol recedit igneus:
Infunde lumen cordibus.
Te mane laudum carmine,
Te deprecamur vespere;
Te nostra supplex gloria
Per cuncta laudet saecula.

14

Blessed Light

Blessed Light of Trinity,
Originating Unity,
Now as the fiery sun declines
Pour radiance in our hearts.
In morning songs we offered praise,
At evening we implore you.
To you, our glory,
Through every age,
May this suppliant offer praise.

Pseudo-Ambrose
4th-5th century

15

ΥΜΝΟΣ ΟΓΔΟΟΣ

Πολυήρατε, κύδιμε,
σέ μάκαρ, γόνε παρθένου
ὑμνῶ Σολυμηίδος,
ὃς τὰν δολίαν πάγαν,
χθόνιον μεγάλων ὄφιν
πατρὸς ἤλασας ὀρχάτων,
ὃς καρπὸν ἀπώμοτον,
τροφὸν ἀργαλέου μόρου,
πόρεν ἀρχεγόνῳ κόρᾳ.
Στεφανηφόρε, κύδιμε,
σέ πάτερ πάι παρθένου
ὑμνῶ Σολυμηίδος·
Κατέβας μέχρι καὶ χθονὸς
ἐπίδημος ἐφαμέροις
βρότεόν τε φέρων δέμας,
κατέβας δ᾿ ὑπὸ Τάρταρα,
ψυχᾶν ὅθι μυρία
θάνατος νέμεν ἔθνεα·
φρίξεν σε γέρων τότε
Ἀίδας ὁ παλαιγενής,
καὶ λαοβόρος κύων,
ὁ βαρυσθενὴς δημοβόρος
ἀνεχάσσατο βηλοῦ.
Λύσας δ᾿ ἀπὸ πημάτων
ψυχᾶν ὁσίους χορούς,
θιάσοις σὺν ἀκηράτοις
ὕμνους ἀνάγεις πατρί.

The Eighth Hymn

I sing to you Most Glorious,
The Blessed One,
Object of our hearts' desire,
Child of the Virgin daughter of Sion;
For from the great gardens of the Father,
You drove the dark Earth Serpent,
That pit of all deceit,
Who offered food,
A painful and unhappy doom,
To the first-born woman.

I sing to you who bear the crown,
Most Glorious,
Child and father
Of the Virgin daughter of Sion.

You came down even to the earth,
To dwell among ephemerals,
And bore a mortal body.
You came down to the depths of Hell,
Since death held in its grip,
The myriad nations of souls.
A shudder, then, of fear
Passed through the aged frame
Of ancient Hades,
As that mighty man-devouring hound
Cringed back into his lair.
You set free the holy choirs of souls
From all their pains,
And brought up hymns to the Father
In that purified and festive company.

Στεφανηφόρε, κύδιμε,
σε πάτερ πάι παρθένου
ὑμνῶ Σολυμηίδος.
Ἀνιόντα σε, κοίρανε,
τὰ κατ᾽ ἠέρος ἄσπετα
τρέσεν ἔθνεα δαιμόνων·
θάμβησε δ᾽ ἀκηράτων
χορὸς ἄμβροτος ἀστέρων·
αἰθὴρ δὲ γελάσσας,
σοφὸς ἁρμονίας πατήρ,
ἐξ ἑπτατόνου λύρας
ἐκεράσσατο μουσικὰν
ἐπινίκιον ἐς μέλος.
Μείδησεν Ἑωσφόρος,
ὁ διάκτορος ἁμέρας,
καὶ χρύσεος Ἕσπερος,
Κυθερήιος ἀστήρ·
ἁ μὲν κερόεν σέλας
πλήσασα ῥόου πυρὸς
ἁγεῖτο Σελάνα,
ποιμὴν νυχίων θεῶν·
τὰν δ᾽ εὐρυφαῆ κόμαν
Τιτὰν ἐπετάσσατο
ἄρρητον ὑπ᾽ ἴχνιον,
ἔγνω δὲ γόνον θεοῦ,
τὸν ἀριστοτέχναν νόον,
ἰδίου πυρὸς ἀρχάν.
Σὺ δὲ ταρσὸν ἐλάσσας
κυανάντυγος οὐρανοῦ
ὑπερήλαο νώτων,
σφαίρῃσι δ᾽ ἐπεστάθης
νοεραῖσιν ἀκηράτοις,
ἀγαθῶν ὅθι παγά,
σιγώμενος οὐρανός.

I sing to you who bear the crown,
Most Glorious,
Child and father
Of the Virgin daughter of Sion.

As you rose on high, O Lord,
The thronging hordes of aerial demons,
Shook with trembling fear.
The immortal choir of
Pure stars of heaven,
Stood, struck with wonder.
The Ether thrilled with joy;
That wise father of all harmony,
Composed a music
On his seven-toned lyre,
For a song of triumph.
The Morning Star was smiling,
The Harbinger of Day,
So too Cytherios the Golden,
The Star of Eventide.
To lead the way the Moon came forth,
Her shining crescent
Brimmed with rippling fire,
The shepherd of the gods of night.
The Titan Sun
Set out his spreading mane
Beneath your awesome feet.
He recognized the Son of God,
Sublime creative mind,
Origin of his own fire.
And you rose high on wings,
Above the azure dome of heaven,
Resting in those Spheres,
Of the Purest Intellect,
Which are the source of every good;
That Heaven of the Silences.

Ἔνθ' οὔτε βαθύρροος
ἀκαμαντοπόδας Χρόνος
χθονὸς ἔκγονα σύρων,
οὐ κῆρες ἀναιδέες
βαθυκύμονος Ὕλας·
ἀλλ' αὐτὸς ἀγήραος
Αἰὼν ὁ παλαιγενής,
νέος ὢν ἅμα καὶ γέρων,
τᾶς ἀενάω μονᾶς
ταμίας πέλεται θεοῖς.

And here Time's tireless tread,
Its ever-pulling current,
That drags along all earthborn kind,
Shall cease to sway.
And here no ruthless Fates
Crash down their waves on Matter.
There is alone that First-Made Age
Beyond all growing old,
ever ancient, ever young,
That holds the eternal mansions
Set aside for gods.

Synesios of Cyrene
4th century

16

Carmen de Christo

Proles vera Dei cunctisque antiquior annis,
Nunc genitus qui semper eras, lucisque repertor,
Ante tuae matrisque parens, quem misit ab astris
Aequaevus genitor, Verbique in semina fusum
Virgineos habitare sinus, et corporis artus
Jussit inire vias, parvaque in sede morari:
Quem sedes non ulla capit, qui lumine primo
Vidisti quidquid mundo nascente creares,
Ipse opifex, opus ipse tui dignatus iniquas
Aetatis sentire vices, et corporis huius
Dissimiles perferre modos, hominemque subire,
Ut posses monstrare Deum, ne lubricus error
Et decepta diu varii solertia mundi
Pectora tam multis sineret mortalia saeclis.
Auctorem scivere Deum te, conscia partus
Mater, et attoniti pecudum sensere timores.
Te nova sollicito lustrantes sidera visu
In coelo videre prius, lumenque secuti
Invenere magi: tu noxia pectora solvis,
Elapsasque animas in corpora functa reducis,
Mundus et ad manes penetras, mortisque latebras
Immortalis adis: tibi tantum non fuit uni
Principium finisve mori, sed nocte refusa
In coelum ad Patrem scandis, rursusque perenni
Ordine purgatis adimis contagia terris.

A Song of Christ

True child of God, more ancient than the years,
Now born who ever were, Deviser of the light,
And parent of your mother,
The Co-eternal Father has sent you from the stars,
Given in that seed which is the Word,
To enter in the Virgin's womb;
Charged to enter in the narrow paths of flesh,
And tarry in so small a seat, whom no place could contain.
Yet in that primal light of the dawning world's new birth
You gazed on all that you had made,
And, Master Craftsman as you are,
You held in honour your own craft,
Suffering this alien form of life,
      to bear the unjust trials of time.
You entered into humankind to show the face of God,
And break the grip that shifting error
Held through many an age, seducing human hearts
By the cleverness of this fickle world.
In the manner of your birth your mother knew you as her God,
Trembling and awed, the beasts sensed their Maker near.
The Magi, searching in the skies, were first to see new stars
Radiant in the heavens, and following the light,
      they came to you.
How gracefully you freed all sinful hearts,
And, where the breath of life had slipped away,
Restored it to bodies that were spent.
You passed Immortal to the Land of Shades,
Breaking in the secret place of death.
You alone shall never die, for flinging back the night
You rose on high to the Father in heaven,
And by your everlasting plan
Purged evil from the face of earth.

Tu solus Patrisque comes, tu Spiritus insons,
Et toties unus, triplicique in lumine simplex.
Quis nisi pro cunctis aliud, quis credere possit
Te potuisse mori, poteras qui reddere vitam?

You alone stand with the Father,
And you the Spirit wholly pure,
Who all are one Simplicity
In the threefold light.
And thus we stand in wonder,
That for our sakes alone,
The holder of the power of life,
Came even to his death.

Flavius Merobaudes
5th century

Carmen Paschale

Christe potens rerum, redeuntis conditor aevi,
Vox summi sensusque Dei: quem fudit ab alta
Mente Pater, tantique dedit consortia regni;
Impia qui nostrae domuisti crimina vitae,
Passus corporea mundi vestire figura,
Affarique palam populos, hominemque fateri:
Quemque utero inclusum Mariae, mox numine viso
Virginei tumuere sinus, innuptaque Mater
Arcano stupuit compleri viscera partu,
Auctorem paritura suum. Mortalia corda
Artificem rexere poli, mundique repertor
Pars fuit humani generis; latuitque sub uno
Pectore qui totum late complectitur orbem;
Et qui non spatiis terrae, non aequoris unda,
Non capitur coelo, parvos confluxit in artus.

A Paschal Hymn

Christ, great Lord of all that is,
Founder of the returning Age,
The voice and thought of God Most High,
Poured from the Father's lofty mind,
Co-Regent of his mighty realm,
You mastered all the evils of our state,
Suffering to be clothed in bodily form.
You chose to address your people face to face,
And be made known as man.
You showed your deity to Mary,
For shut within her womb,
You swelled her virgin flesh.
The unwed mother stood in awe
To be so big with child
From this arcane conception;
To bring forth Him who fashioned her.
Mortal hearts held sway over the maker of the Heavens
As the world's creator first entered humankind.
His embrace reaches all around the spreading orb,
Yet now he lies beneath a rounded breast,
And hides in cramping flesh,
Though no vast space on earth,
Or in the ocean's depths,
Or through the very heavens,
Could ever close Him in.

Quin et supplicii nomen, nexusque subisti,
Ut nos subriperes letho, mortemque fugares
Morte tua: mox aethereas evectus in auras,
Purgata repetis laetum tellure parentem.
Angustum foveas, festis ut saepe diebus
Annua sinceri celebret jejunia sacri.

But more than this,
You came to plead, in debt,
To snatch us out of death,
And by your death put death to flight.
Having purged the earth of sin
How high you rose upon celestial airs,
Returning as your Father's joy.
Give comfort now to this poor man
That in recurring festal days
He may keep the the yearly fasts
Of this most pure solemnity.

Flavius Merobaudes
5th century

Hymnus Ante Cibum

O crucifer bone, lucisator,
Omniparens, pie, verbigena,
Edite corpore virgineo,
Sed prius in genitore potens,
Astra, solum, mare quam fierent:

Huc nitido precor intuitu
Flecte salutiferam faciem,
Fronte serenus et inradia,
Nominis ut sub honore tui
Has epulas liceat capere.

Te sine dulce nihil, Domine,
Nec iuvat ore quid adpetere,
Pocula ni prius atque cibos,
Christe, tuus favor inbuerit
Omnia sanctificante fide.

Fercula nostra Deum sapiant,
Christus et influat in pateras:
Seria, ludicra, verba, iocos,
Denique quod sumus aut agimus,
Trina superne regat pietas.

18

A Hymn Before Eating

Kind Lord who bore the cross,
Source of all our light,
All-creative, gracious, Word-begot,
Now made flesh within the Virgin's womb,
Yet mighty in your Father, first,
Before the stars, or earth, or seas were made,

Turn your saving face, I pray,
Upon this fertile scene,
That with your peace, and in your light,
And under your ennobling name,
We may enjoy this food.

Without you, Lord, nothing is sweet;
Whatever we eat dissatisfies;
Unless our food and drink
Are savoured first, by sanctifying faith,
Tinged with Christ's own favour.

So let our simple bread bear the taste of God.
May Christ flow within our cups.
May the threefold holiness above
Direct our sober words, and jests,
Our laughter and our talk,
Whatever we do, and all we are.

Haec opulentia Christicolis
Servit et omnia suppeditat:
Absit enim procul illa fames,
Caedibus ut pecudum libeat
Sanguineas lacerare dapes.

Sint fera gentibus indomitis
Prandia de nece quadrupedum:
Nos oleris coma, nos siliqua
Feta legumine multimodo
Paverit innocuis epulis.

Such opulence, for Christians, is enough,
And satisfies all needs.
Far from us be that hungering lust
That craves a bloody feast
And tears apart the flesh of beasts.

Such wild banquets made from slaughtered flocks,
Are fit for barbarians alone;
For us the olive, wheat, and ripening fruits,
And vegetables of every kind.
These make up our righteous feast.

Prudentius
5th century

19

Hymnus Ad Incensum Lucernae

Inventor rutili, dux bone, luminis,
Qui certis vicibus tempora dividis,
Merso sole chaos ingruit horridum,
Lucem redde tuis Christe fidelibus.

Quamvis innumero sidere regiam
Lunarique polum lampade pinxeris,
Incussu silicis lumina nos tamen
Monstras saxigeno semine quaerere:

Ne nesciret homo spem sibi luminis
In Christi solido corpore conditam,
Qui dici stabilem se voluit petram,
Nostris igniculis unde genus venit.

Pinguis quos olei rore madentibus
Lychnis aut facibus pascimus aridis:
Quin et fila favis scirpea floreis
Presso melle prius conlita fingimus.

Vivax flamma viget, seu cava testula
Sucum linteolo suggerit ebrio,
Seu pinus piceam fert alimoniam,
Seu ceram teretem stuppa calens bibit.

Hymn at the Lighting of the Lamps

Gracious Lord, Creator of the golden light,
You establish the patterns of revolving time,
And as the sun now sets, the gloom of night advances in.
For all your faithful, Christ, restore the light.

You have arrayed your heavenly court
With all the countless stars,
    setting the moon there as a lamp,
Yet still have shown us how to seek
Those lights whose seeds spring out
Whenever stony flint is struck.

This was to teach mankind its hope,
That light bestowed on us
When Christ came with his own flesh.
For as he said, He is that steadfast rock,
From which a fire sprang forth to all our race.

This tiny flame we nurse in lamps
Brimming with rich and fragrant oil,
Or on the dry timber of the torch,
Or on the rushlights we have made,
Steeped in wax pressed from the comb.

The flickering light grows strong,
As the hollow earthware lamp
    yields up its richness to the thirsty wick,
As the pine branch drips its nourishing sap,
And the fire drinks the warmth of waxen tapers down.

Nectar de liquido vertice fervidum
Guttatim lacrimis stillat olentibus,
Ambustum quoniam vis facit ignea
Imbrem de madido flere cacumine.

Splendent ergo tuis muneribus, Pater,
Flammis mobilibus scilicet atria,
Absentemque diem lux agit aemula,
Quam nox cum lacero victa fugit peplo.

* * * * * *

Tu lux vera oculis, lux quoque sensibus,
Intus tu speculum, tu speculum foris,
Lumen, quod famulans offero, suscipe,
Tinctum pacifici chrismatis unguine.

Per Christum genitum, summe Pater, tuum,
In quo visibilis stat tibi gloria,
Qui noster Dominus, qui tuus unicus
Spirat de patrio corde Paraclitum,

Per quem splendor, honos, laus, sapientia,
Maiestas, bonitas, et pietas tua,
Regnum continuat numine triplici
Texens perpetuis saecula saeculis.

Drop by drop in perfumed tears
The glowing liquid nectar falls.
The eager fire sends forth rain
As burning waxen candles weep themselves away.

It is by your own gifts, Father,
Our halls are gleaming now with dancing lights
That strive to emulate departed day,
While conquered night withdraws in flight,
Rending her dark cloak as she goes.

Lord, you are the true light of our eyes,
And light to all our senses;
That which we see within, and that which lies without.
Accept this light I offer you, as my worship, Lord;
A light that brims, with perfumed oils of peace.

Most Holy Father, through Christ your Son,
Your glory stands revealed,
Your Only Born, Our Lord,
Who breathed the Spirit over us,
Out of the bosom of the Father;

Through him your glory, honour, praise, and wisdom;
Your goodness, gracefulness, and might,
Endure in your kingdom, thrice holy God,
And spread through Ages of everlasting Ages. Amen.

Prudentius
5th century

20

ΕΥΧΗ ΕΠ' ΑΡΙΣΤΩ

Εὐλογητὸς εἶ, Κύριε,
ὁ τρέφων με ἐκ νεότητός μου,
ὁ διδοὺς τροφὴν πάσῃ σαρκί
Πλήρωσον χαρᾶς καὶ εὐφροσύνης τὰς καρδίας ἡμῶν,
ἵνα πάντοτε πᾶσαν αὐτάρκειαν ἔχοντες
περισσεύωμεν εἰς πᾶν ἔργον ἀγαθὸν
ἐν Χριστῷ Ἰησοῦ τῷ κυρίῳ ἡμῶν·
μεθ' οὗ σοι δόξα, τιμὴ καὶ κράτος
εἰς τοὺς αἰῶνας. Ἀμήν.

A Grace Before Eating

Blessed are you, O Lord,
who have fed me from my youth,
and give all flesh their food.
Fill our hearts with joy and gladness,
That having all we need,
We might abound in all good works
In Christ Jesus our Lord;
With whom to you be glory, honour,
    and dominion,
Unto the Ages. Amen.

Byzantine Anonymous
circa 5th century

21

ΥΜΝΟΣ ΕΣΠΕΡΙΟΣ

Δέξαι φωνάς, οὐράνιε
τρισάγιε σωτὴρ ἡμῶν,
ὑπὸ ἡμῶν τῶν ἐπὶ γῆς
ἐστώτων καὶ ὑμνούντων σε·
τῷ ἀκοιμήτῳ ὄμματι
ἐπίβλεψον, φιλάνθρωπε,
εἰς τὴν ἡμῶν ἀσθένειαν,
καὶ δὸς ἡμῖν κατάνυξιν·
δέξαι τὴν προσευχὴν ἡμῶν,
καὶ ἄνες ταῖς ψυχαῖς ἡμῶν,
μὴ ματαιώσωσιν ἡμῶν
ἁμαρτίαι τὴν δέησιν·
τοῦ ὀδυρμοῦ τῆς κρίσεως
ῥῦσαι ἡμᾶς τοὺς δούλους σου
καὶ τοῦ χοροῦ τῶν ἁγίων
ἀξίωσον τοὺς ψάλλοντας·
Δόξα πατρὶ καὶ τῷ υἱῷ
καὶ τῷ ἁγίῳ πνεύματι
εἰς τοὺς αἰῶνας τῶν αἰώνων. ἀμήν.

A Hymn at Eventide

Receive the prayers,
Thrice Holy Saviour,
Of those who stand on earth and hymn you.
Look down with sleepless eye,
O Lover of the human race,
And overlook our weakness,
And grant us peaceful rest.
Receive our prayer,
Raise up our souls,
Lest our sins
Frustrate our prayer.
Deliver us, your servants,
From the grief of Judgement,
And make us worthy,
Who sing to you now,
To stand in the chorus of saints.
Glory to the Father,
And to the Son,
And to the Holy Spirit,
Unto the Ages of Ages.   Amen.

Byzantine Anonymous
Late 5th Century

22

ΥΜΝΟΣ ΤΟΥ ΕΣΠΕΡΙΝΟΥ

Ἡ ἀσώματος φύσις τῶν Χερουβὶμ
ἀσιγήτοις σε ὕμνοις δοξολογεῖ ·
ἐξαπτέρυγα ζῷα, τὰ Σεραφίμ,
ταῖς ἀπαύστοις φωναῖς σε ὑπερυψοῖ·
τῶν ἀγγέλων δὲ πᾶσαι αἱ στρατιαὶ
τρισαγίοις σε ᾄσμασιν εὐφημεῖ·
πρὸ γὰρ πάντων ὑπάρχεις ὁ ὢν πατὴρ
καὶ συνάναρχον ἔχεις τὸν υἱόν,
καὶ ἰσότιμον φέρων πνεῦμα ζωῆς
τῆς τριάδος δεικνύεις τὸ ἀμερές.
Παναγία παρθένε, μήτηρ Χριστοῦ,
οἱ τοῦ λόγου αὐτόπται καὶ ὑπουργοί,
προφητῶν καὶ μαρτύρων πάντες χοροὶ
ὡς ἀθάνατον ἔχοντες τὴν ζωήν,
ὑπὲρ πάντων πρεσβεύσατε ἱλασμόν,
ὅτι πάντες ὑπάρχομεν ἐν δεινοῖς·
τῆς δὲ πλάνης ῥυσθέντες τοῦ πονηροῦ
τῶν ἀγγέλων βοήσωμεν τὴν ᾠδήν.

22

An Evening Hymn

The bodiless nature of the Cherubim
Glorifies you with ceaseless hymns.
The six-winged Living Ones, the Seraphim,
Exalt you with unwearied cries.
All the rank on rank of angels,
Praise you with thrice-holy song.

Father, existing before all,
With your Co-Eternal Son,
And Spirit of Life,
All equal in honour,
You show forth
Undividedness of Trinity.

All Holy Virgin, Mother of Christ,
Servants and Eye-witnesses of the Word,
The whole chorus of Prophets and Martyrs,
Enjoying the Immortal Life,
Intercede for mercy on us all,
As all of us are in distress.

Let us be delivered from the
Deceit of the Evil One,
And sing out the Song of Angels.

Byzantine Anonymous
Late 5th century

A Moral Palindrome

Wash off your evil deeds,
Don't just wash your face.

Byzantine Anonymous
circa 6th century

Η ΤΟΥ ΤΑΠΕΙΝΟΥ ΡΩΜΑΝΟΥ ΥΜΝΟΣ.

Ἡ παρθένος σήμερον
τὸν ὑπερούσιον τίκτει,
καὶ ἡ γῆ τὸ σπήλαιον
τῷ ἀπροσίτῳ προσάγει·
ἄγγελοι μετὰ ποιμένων δοξολογοῦσι,
μάγοι δὲ μετὰ ἀστέρος ὁδοιποροῦσι·
δι᾿ ἡμᾶς γὰρ ἐγεννήθη
παιδίον νέον
ὁ πρὸ αἰώνων θεός.

α´
Τὴν Ἐδὲμ Βηθλεὲμ
ἤνοιξε, δεῦτε ἴδωμεν·
τὴν τρυφὴν ἐν κρυφῇ
ηὕραμεν, δεῦτε λάβωμεν
τὰ τοῦ παραδείσου
ἐντὸς τοῦ σπηλαίου·
ἐκεῖ ἐφάνη ῥίζα ἀπότιστος
βλαστάνουσα ἄφεσιν,
ἐκεῖ ηὑρέθη φρέαρ ἀνόρυκτον,
οὗ πιεῖν Δαβὶδ πρὶν ἐπεθύμησεν·
ἐκεῖ παρθένος τεκοῦσα βρέφος
τὴν δίψαν ἔπαυσεν εὐθὺς
τὴν τοῦ Ἀδὰμ καὶ τοῦ Δαβίδ·
διὰ τοῦτο πρὸς τοῦτο
ἐπειχθῶμεν, ποῦ ἐτέχθη
παιδίον νέον,
ὁ πρὸ αἰώνων θεός.

A Christmas Hymn

The Virgin this day gives birth
To One beyond all nature.
And Earth draws in, offering a cave
To One who cannot be approached.
Angels with shepherds give glory
And Magi make their way,
By following after a star;
For there is born to us
    a tiny child
    who is God before all times began.

Bethlehem reopens Eden's gate.
Come let us behold.
What delights we have found hidden here.
Come, and take
Gifts of Paradise from within a cave.
There we saw an unwatered root
Budding forth forgiveness.
There we found the still-sealed well
From which David had long aspired to drink.
There was a Virgin who, by giving birth to a child,
Straightway quenched the thirst,
Not only of David, but of Adam too.
And so to this we came,
To see the birthplace of
    a tiny child,
    who is God before all times began.

στ´
Παραδόξων ῥητῶν
ἡ Μαριὰμ ὡς ἤκουσε,
τῷ ἐκ σπλάγχνων αὐτῆς
κρύψασα προσεκύνησε
καὶ κλαίουσα εἶπε·
Μεγάλα μοι τέκνον,
μεγάλα πάντα, ὅσα ἐποίησας
μετὰ τῆς πτωχείας μου·
ἰδοὺ γὰρ μάγοι
ἔξω ζητοῦσί σε
τῶν ἀνατολῶν οἱ βασιλεύοντες·
τὸ πρόσωπόν σου ἐπιζητοῦσι
καὶ λιτανεύουσιν ἰδεῖν
οἱ πλούσιοι τοῦ σοῦ λαοῦ·
ὁ λαός σου γὰρ ὄντως
εἰσὶν οὗτοι, οἷς ἐγνώσθης
παιδίον νέον
ὁ πρὸ αἰώνων θεός.

When Mary heard these wondrous words,
Secretly she worshipped the child of her womb,
Weeping as she says: 'How mighty, my child,
How mighty the things which you have wrought,
Out of this poverty of mine;
For see the Magi outside, the Kings of the East,
                              who seek you.
The wealthy among your people
Seek, and pray to see, your face.'
For your people are indeed those to whom
You are made known: a child newborn,
Yet God before all ages.

Romanos the Singer
6th century

25

ΣΤΙΧΗΡΑ ΑΝΑΣΤΑΣΙΜΑ

ά

Τὰς ἑσπερινὰς ἡμῶν εὐχὰς
πρόσδεξαι, ἅγιε, Κύριε,
καὶ παράσχου ἡμῖν
ἄφεσιν ἁμαρτιῶν,
ὅτι μόνος εἶ ὁ δείξας
ἐν κόσμῳ τὴν ἀνάστασιν.
Κυκλώσατε, λαοὶ Σιὼν
καὶ περιλάβετε αὐτήν,
καὶ δότε δόξαν ἐν αὐτῇ
τῷ ἀναστάντι ἐκ νεκρῶν,
ὅτι αὐτός ἐστιν ὁ θεὸς ἡμῶν,
ὁ λυτρωσάμενος ἡμᾶς,
ἐκ τῶν ἀνομιῶν ἡμῶν.
Δεῦτε, λαοί, ὑμνήσωμεν
καὶ προσκυνήσωμεν Χριστόν,
δοξάζοντες αὐτοῦ
τὴν ἐκ νεκρῶν ἀνάστασιν,
ὅτι αὐτός ἐστιν ὁ θεὸς ἡμῶν,
ὁ ἐκ τῆς πλάνης τοῦ ἐχθροῦ
τὸν κόσμον λυτρωσάμενος.

Hymns on the Resurrection

Most Holy Lord,
Receive our evening prayers,
And grant to us
Forgiveness of our sins.
None else but you
Has shown within this world,
The Resurrection.

'Go round Sion, you peoples,
And encircle her,'
Give glory in her
To Him who rose from the dead,
Who is Himself our very God;
For from the midst of all our sins,
He has redeemed us all.

Come, my people,
Let us sing a hymn,
Venerating Christ,
To glorify his Resurrection
From the dead.
He is our very God
And has redeemed the world
From all the Enemy's deceit.

St John of Damascus
8th century

26

ΣΤΙΧΗΡΑ ΑΝΑΣΤΑΣΙΜΑ
ΘΕΟΤΟΚΙΟΝ

Τὴν παγκόσμιον δόξαν,
τὴν ἐξ ἀνθρώπων σπαρεῖσαν
καὶ τὸν δεσπότην τεκοῦσαν,
τὴν ἐπουράνιον πύλην
ὑμνήσωμεν Μαρίαν τὴν παρθένον,
τῶν ἀσωμάτων τὸ ἆσμα
καὶ τῶν πιστῶν τὸ ἐγκαλλώπισμα·
αὕτη γὰρ ἀνεδείχθη
οὐρανὸς
καὶ ναὸς τῆς θεότητος·
αὕτη τὸ μεσότοιχον
τῆς ἔχθρας καθελοῦσα
εἰρήνην ἀντεισῆξε
καὶ τὸ βασίλειον ἠνέωξε·
ταύτην οὖν κατέχοντες
τῆς πίστεως τὴν ἄγκυραν
ὑπέρμαχον ἔχομεν
τὸν ἐξ αὐτῆς τεχθέντα κύριον·
θαρσεῖτε τοίνυν, θαρσεῖτε, λαὸς τοῦ θεοῦ·
καὶ γὰρ αὐτὸς πολεμήσει
τοὺς ἐχθροὺς ὡς φιλάνθρωπος.

Hymn to the Virgin

Let us sing a hymn
To Mary the Virgin,
That Heavenly Gate
And glory of our world,
The new bud of humankind
That gave birth to the Lord.

Of her the angels make their song,
The proud boast of all the Church,
For she received within herself
No less than heaven,
The temple of our God.

And she has broken down
The dividing-wall of enmity;
Has brought about our peace,
Opened access to the throne of God.

Hold fast to her,
The anchor of our faith.
We have as mighty champion,
Her who from her very self
Gave to the Lord his birth.

And so take heart,
Take heart you people of God,
For he himself shall gird for war
Against our many foes,
Who is the Lover of Mankind.

St John of Damascus
8th century

27

ΣΤΙΧΗΡΑ ΑΝΑΣΤΑΣΙΜΑ

β´

Τὸν ζωοποιόν σου σταυρὸν
ἀπαύστως προσκυνοῦντες, Χριστὲ ὁ θεός,
τὴν τριήμερόν σου ἀνάστασιν δοξάζομεν·
δί αὐτῆς γὰρ ἀνεκαίνισας
τὴν καταφθαρεῖσαν τῶν ἀνθρώπων
φύσιν, παντοδύναμε,
καὶ τὴν εἰς οὐρανοὺς ἄνοδον
καθυπέδειξας ἡμῖν,
ὡς μόνος ἀγαθὸς καὶ φιλάνθρωπος.

Hymn to the Life-Giving Cross

Ceaselessly we bow,
O Christ our God,
Before your Cross
That gives us Life;
And glorify your Resurrection,
Most Powerful Lord,
When on that third day
You made anew
The failing nature of Mankind,
Showing us so clearly
The way back to heaven above:
For you alone are Good,
The Lover of Mankind.

St John of Damascus
8th century

28

ΙΔΙΟΜΕΛΟΝ ΕΙΣ ΤΗΝ ΥΠΑΠΑΝΤΗΝ ΤΟΥ ΧΡΙΣΤΟΥ

δ´

'Ανοιγέσθω ἡ πύλη τοῦ οὐρανοῦ σήμερον·
ὁ γὰρ ἄναρχος λόγος τοῦ πατρὸς,
ἀρχὴν λαβὼν χρονικὴν,
μὴ ἐκστὰς τῆς αὐτοῦ θεότητος,
ὑπὸ παρθένου ὡς βρέφος
τεσσαρακονθήμερον
μητρὸς ἑκὼν προσφέρεται
ἐν ναῷ τῷ νομικῷ·
καὶ τοῦτον ἀγκάλαις εἰσδέχεται ὁ πρέσβυς,
ἀπόλυσον, κράζων, τὸν δοῦλον ὁ δεσπότης·
οἱ γὰρ ὀφθαλμοί μου
εἶδον τὸ σωτήριόν σου·
ὁ ἐλθὼν εἰς τὸν κόσμον
σῶσαι γένος ἀνθρώπων·
κύριε, δόξα σοι.

Hymn on the Presentation of the Lord

Today let the gate of Heaven be opened up,
For the Father's Word, without beginning,
Who has taken a beginning in Time,
Though never seceding from his deity,
Is, in the arms of his virgin mother,
A child of merely forty days,
Willingly carried into the Temple of the Law.

The old man received him in his arms,
Crying out: 'Master, dismiss your servant,
For my eyes have seen your salvation.'

Glory to you, O Lord,
Who have come into the world
To save all human kind.

St John of Damascus
8th century

29

Carmen Paschale

Surrexit Christus sol verus vespere noctis,
Surgit et hinc domini mystica messis agri.
Nunc vaga puniceis apium plebs laeta labore
Floribus instrepitans poblite mella legit.
Nunc variae volucres permulcent aethera cantu,
Temperat et pernox nunc philomela melos.
Nunc chorus ecclesiae cantat per cantica Sion,
Alleluia suis centuplicatque tonis.
Tado, pater patriae, caelestis gaudia paschae
Percipias meritis limina lucis: Ave.

A Paschal Song

Christ, our True Sun,
    last night from darkness rose,
And in the Lord's fields,
    the mystic harvest now is springing up.
The wandering clans of bees,
    happy in their chores,
Murmur far through scarlet flowers,
    gathering their honey about.
How many birds now soften the air with melody,
And as dusk falls the nightingale
    modulates her song,
While in the church
    the choir chants hymns of Sion,
And in its various modes
    sings Alleluias hundredfold.
Tado, father of your people,
    the joys of this celestial Pasch,
    the threshold of the light,
Are rightly yours. All Hail.

Sedulius Scotus
9th century

30

ΙΔΙΟΜΕΛΑ ΕΙΣ ΤΗΝ ΧΡΙΣΤΟΥ ΓΕΝΝΗΣΙΝ

Εὐφραίνεσθε δίκαιοι,
οὐρανιοὶ ἀγαλλιᾶσθε,
σκιρτήσατε τὰ ὄρη
Χριστοῦ γεννηθέντος·
παρθένος καθέζεται
τὰ Χερουβὶν μιμουμένη,
βαστάζουσα ἐν κόλποις
θεὸν λόγον σαρκωθέντα·
ποιμένες τὸν τεχθέντα δοξάζουσι,
μάγοι τῷ δεσπότῃ δῶρα προσφέρουσιν·
ἄγγελοι ἀνυμνοῦντες λέγουσιν·
ἀκατάληπτε κύριε, δόξα σοι.

Ὁ Πατὴρ ηὐδόκησεν,
ὁ λόγος σὰρξ ἐγένετο,
καὶ ἡ παρθένος ἔτεκεν
θεὸν ἐνανθρωπήσαντα·
ἀστὴρ μηνύει,
μάγοι προσκυνοῦσιν,
ποιμένες θαυμάζουσι,
καὶ ἡ κτίσις ἀγάλλεται.

Θεοτόκε παρθένε,
ἡ τεκοῦσα τὸν σωτῆρα,
ἀνέτρεψας τὴν πρώτην κατάραν τῆς Εὔας,
ὅτι μήτηρ γέγονας
τῆς εὐδοκίας τοῦ πατρός,
βαστάζουσα ἐν κόλποις
θεὸν λόγον σαρκωθέντα·
οὐ φέρει τὸ μυστήριον ἔρευναν,
πίστει μόνῃ τοῦτο πάντες δοξάζομεν,
κράζοντες μετὰ σοῦ καὶ λέγοντες·
ἀνερμήνευτε κύριε, δόξα σοι·

Verses on the Birth of Christ

You righteous rejoice,
You heavens be glad,
You mountains leap for joy!
For Christ is born.
The Virgin sits,
Like the very Cherubim,
Holding in her lap
God the Word made flesh.
The shepherds worship the newborn child,
The Magi offer gifts to their Lord.
The angels sing a hymn and say:
'Incomprehensible Lord: Glory to You.'

The Father is well-pleased.
The Word has been made flesh.
The Virgin gives birth,
To God the Word made man.
A star discloses it.
The Magi fall in adoration,
The shepherds stand in awe,
As the whole of creation rejoices.

Virgin Mother of God
You brought forth your Saviour,
Overturning the ancient curse of Eve,
For you became the mother
Of the Father's own delight,
Bearing in your lap
God the Word made flesh.
This mystery is beyond conception,
By faith alone we honour it,
Crying out along with you:
'Incomprehensible Lord: Glory to You.'

Δεῦτε ἀνυμνήσωμεν τὴν μητέρα τοῦ σωτῆρος
τὴν μετὰ τόκον πάλιν ὀφθεῖσαν παρθένον·
χαίροις, πόλις ἔμψυχε τοῦ βασιλέως καὶ θεοῦ,
ἐν ᾗ Χριστὸς οἰκήσας σωτηρίαν εἰργάσατο·
μετὰ τοῦ Γαβριὴλ ἀνυμνοῦμέν σε,
μετὰ τῶν ποιμένων δοξάζομεν κράζοντες·
Θεοτόκε, πρέσβευε τῷ ἐκ σοῦ σαρκωθέντι
σωθῆναι ἡμᾶς.

Come, let us sing to the Mother of the Saviour,
Even after childbirth, Virgin still we own her.
Rejoice, Living City of our King and God,
In which Christ dwelling, worked out our salvation.
  With Gabriel we hymn you;
  With the shepherds we glorify you, crying:
  'Mother of God, intercede with him made flesh of you,
  That he might save us.'

Andrew of Jerusalem
7th-8th century

31

ΓΕΩΡΓΙΟΙΟ ΑΛΙΤΡΟΙΟ ΥΜΝΟΣ

Μνώεο, Χριστέ,
υἱὲ θεοῖο
ὑψιμέδοντος,
οἰκέτεω σέο
κῆρ ἀλιτροῖο
γράψαντος τάδε·
καί μοι ὄπασσον
λῦσιν παθέων
κηριτρεφέων
τά μοι ἐμφύει
ψυχᾷ ῥυπαρᾷ·
δὸς δὲ ἰδέσθαι,
σῶτερ Ἰησοῦ,
ζαθέαν αἴγλαν
σάν· ἔνθα φανεὶς
μέλψω ἀοιδὰν
ψυχᾶν παίονι,
παίονι γυίων
πατρὶ σὺν μεγάλῳ
πνεύματι θ᾽ ἀγνῷ.

The Prayer of the Scribe

Be mindful, Christ,
And Son of God,
Enthroned on High,
Of this your sinful servant,
Who transcribes all these poems,
And grant to me,
Release from passions,
That feed so many griefs,
But are so deeply rooted,
in my sinful soul.
Jesus, Saviour,
Grant me sight
Of all your sacred splendour.
For in that vision
I shall sing so sweet a song
To the Healer of Souls,
To the Healer of the lame,
Together with the Mighty Father,
And the Holy Spirit.   Amen.

Pseudo-Synesios (George the Sinner)
10th century

NOTES

1. The Gospel of John, 1:1-5, 9-14, 16-18.

To read Sirach 24:1-17 in parallel with the Johannine Prologue reveals its inner dynamic as a hymn about God's salvation of his elect people. In John's text the Logos mysticism of Philo which had been referred to the Pre-existent Torah, or Wisdom of God, is specified as the Incarnate Lord. Thus Jesus is identified by the text as the heart of the covenantal salvation offered by God to his people, and election is founded upon faith in his name. The Wisdom of God in Sirach 24 searches around to find somewhere to pitch her tent. The triumphant assertion of John 1:14 is that this Wisdom at last 'pitched its tent' or dwelt among us, when made flesh. The stress on incarnation marks The Prologue off at once from Philonic or Gnostic approaches to theology. See R. Brown, *The Gospel According to St John*, Anchor Bible Commentaries, London, 1984, pp.3-37; including bibliography, op. cit. pp.36-37.

2. Letter of Paul to the Philippians, 2:5-11.

Cf. R. P. Martin, *New Century Bible Commentaries*, London, 1989, pp.90-102; Ibid. *Carmen Christi: Phil. 2:5-11 in Recent Interpretation and in the Setting of Early Christian Worship*, Cambridge, 1967; M. Hooker, *From Adam to Christ*, Cambridge, 1990, pp.88-100; J. Jervell, *Imago Dei*, Gottingen, 1960, pp.206-209 (arguing a Baptismal setting for the hymn); J. T. Sanders, *The NT Christological Hymns*, Cambridge, 1971, pp.66-69.

3. Letter of Paul to the Colossians, 1:15-20.

Read Ephesians 1:3-14 in parallel with this hymn for a similarly cosmic view of Christ's redemptive work. Cf. P. T. O'Brien, *Colossians and Philemon*, Word Bible Commentaries, Vol. 44, Waco, Texas, 1982; Bibliography, op. cit. pp.31-32.

4. First Letter of Paul to Timothy, 3:16.

The opening subject of the hymn is stated in the original scribal hand of the main manuscript (Sinaiticus) as 'He who' (*ós*), a reading which is followed by Origen. The corrected scribal version 'e' of Sinaiticus reads: 'God' (*theos*), which is followed by Gregory Nyssa and the Byzantine Lectionary. It seems likely that in the process of citing the hymn the original subject referent has been grammatically altered and now is impossible to recall, although it was obviously referring to the incarnate Lord, not, as some have rendered it, looking back to the last neuter subject of the text, i.e. 'the mystery of faith'. It might well have been another Logos hymn, as many of its concerns mirror those of John 1:14. In Timothy the text bears the character of a summary credal confession. Cf. R. Falconer, *The Pastoral Epistles*, Oxford, 1937; J. N. D. Kelly, *A Commentary on the Pastoral Epistles*, NY, 1963.

5.   The Book of Revelation, 15:3-4.

For the original song of Moses see Exodus 15:1-18; Deut. 32:1-43. The typology of the Exodus underlies the whole format of this liturgical canticle. The victory of the Lamb is presented in this section of the book as the culmination of all the redemptive acts of God for his people since the liberation from bondage in Egypt. This last of the great works of redemption is that which also rolls up the course of history, inaugurating the end times. The hymn is a blending of many acclamations from the Psalms and other fragments of the OT, a composition from a mind steeped in the scriptures; see Ps. 86:9; 111:2; 139:14; 145:17; Deut. 32:4; Jer. 10:7. Cf. T. F. Glasson, *The Revelation of John*, Cambridge, 1965.

6.   *Hymn to Christ the Shepherd*, Clement of Alexandria.

Clement (*circa* 150-215) was probably an Athenian by birth and succeeded Pantaenus as the leading Christian *didaskalos* in Alexandria in about 190. His works are in *PG* 8-9; Critical edition by O. Stahlin, *Griechischen Christlichen Schriftstellen*, Vols. 1-3, 1905-9; French translation of the 'Pedagogus' in Vols. 70 and 108 of the *Sources Chrétiennes* series, eds. M. Harl and C. Mondesert, Paris, 1960f. For a general appreciation cf. C. Bigg, *The Christian Platonists of Alexandria*; Bibliographies, etc., cf. Quasten, Vol. 2, pp.5-36. Text: Christ-Paranikas, pp.37-8 (line 3 emended).

7. *Hail Gladdening Light*, from the Byzantine Liturgy of evening.

In Byzantine timekeeping, the advent of evening marked the new day, and the vigils of the feasts were begun. This hymn was sung as the lamps of evening were first lit. Text: Christ-Paranikas, p.40.

8. *The Cherubic Hymn*, from the Byzantine Liturgy.

This famous hymn is sung at the Great Entrance during the Byzantine Eucharistic liturgy. Its few words belie its significant length when sung. It has been said that the choir of Hagia Sophia in ancient Byzantium numbered several eunuchs who, being sexless, particularly 'imaged' the angels, and in their highly pitched singing rendered this chant as an eerie evocation of the angels descending with their Lord like imperial warriors attending the Emperor. Text: *The Sunday Services* (Gk), edited by T. Matthaiake (Athens 1985), p.390.

9. *Eucharistic Hymn*, from the Byzantine Liturgy.

The emphasis on the secrecy of the mysteries of Christianity, a very ancient theme, is still dominant here. In the ancient liturgy before the mysteries were celebrated the catechumens were expelled. It is a charming biblical construct, a confession and prayer for forgiveness before the taking of communion. Text: *The Great Horologion.*

10. *The Great Akathist to the Mother of God*, from the Byzantine Liturgy (possibly by Romanos the Singer, and edited by Patriarch Sergius).

For the question of its much controverted authorship see Wellesz. Patriarch Sergius traditionally added the Proem in celebration of a defeat of enemy armies at the very walls of Constantinople, a victory attributed to the Virgin's intercession to save the city that had been dedicated to her. The title *akathist* means 'not sitting down'; in other words it was a processional hymn of celebration. It is sung complete in the Lenten services of the Byzantine Rite. This represents only the opening stanzas. Text: Trypanis, pp.9-10.

11. *Hymn of Thanksgiving*, St Gregory Nazianzen.

Gregory (*circa* 329-389) was one of the Cappadocian Fathers, a friend of Basil and Gregory Nyssa, the teacher of Evagrius of Pontike, and cousin of Amphilocius of Iconium. He is also called one of the Three Holy Hierarchs of the Eastern Church, but more commonly called Gregory the Theologian in the Eastern tradition, to signify the high regard in which his work has always been held. He was the great defender of the deity of Christ in the period of late Arianism at the end of the fourth century. At the Council of Constantinople in 381, along with Gregory Nyssa, he was one of the leading architects of the Christian doctrine of the Trinity. In his final years in retirement he dedicated his time to literature, being convinced in the aftermath of the Emperor Julian's attacks on Christianity that it was necessary to assert the Church's right to express Roman civilised values in a distinctively Christian culture. His feast days are on January 25th and 30th. Bibliography: Quasten, Vol. 3, pp.236-54, esp. pp.245-6.

Werhahn has raised some doubts over this hymn and others in this section of Theological Hymns (31-5, 37, 38). His queries do not seem sufficiently strong to compel us to regard it as spurious. Its style, diction and general theological manner are in perfect harmony with the unquestionably genuine hymns of Gregory. Text: Theological Hymns, 1,1,34; *PG* 37, 515-17.

12. *A Hymn at Dawn*, St Ambrose of Milan.

Ambrose (*circa* 339-397) was born at Trier, the son of the Praetorian Prefect of Gaul. He practised as a lawyer and rose to high civic rank until, in 370, he was appointed Roman Governor of the Province of Aemilia Liguria with his official seat at Milan. The Milanese bishop Auxentius was one of the leading Arians of the day, and at his death in 374 the catholic population of Milan acclaimed Ambrose as his successor, for even though he was not yet baptized, he was known to have catholic views. His friend and tutor was the priest Simplicianus, one of the leaders of the catholic party in the church of that city. Once ordained, Ambrose was taught theology by Simplicianus and soon became one of the greatest of all the Western bishops, influencing Augustine considerably. With Jerome, Augustine and Gregory the Great, he is regarded as one of the four 'Doctors' of the Latin Church. He is commonly regarded as the founding father of Latin hymnography, introducing the practice of religious hymnody into the church of Milan from his knowledge of Eastern Christian practice. His feast day is December 7th. Ambrose was an indefatigable worker, often spending the night hours in reading and prayer. Such a man was well accustomed to hearing the cock-crow, and it moved him to write one of the most famous of all Latin hymns. Text: Hymn 1, *PL* 16, 1409.

13. *Christ, Splendour of the Father's Glory*, St Ambrose of Milan.

The final two lines of the poem represent Ambrose's manner of teaching his people, by means of hymns, the Nicene doctrine of the full deity of the Son of God, in opposition to Arianism which was still rife in the Church of his day. Text: Hymn 7, *PL* 16, 1414.

14. *O Blessed Light*, Pseudo Ambrose (4th-5th Century?).

Ambrose's reputation as the father of Latin hymnody attracted to him a large body of 'attributions'. Many of them are pastiches of his distinctive Latin style of regular rhythmic lines that lend themselves to choral recitation, but several of them are works of art in their own right. This is an example of the terse rigour that Latin can command in epitomising abstract concepts in a highly memorable way. It shows the hymn at its most effective catechetical level. Text: Hymn 11, *PL* 16, 1412.

15. *The Eighth Hymn*, Synesios of Cyrene.

Synesios was born at Cyrene in Libya sometime between 370 and 375. No further writings are found from him after 413. He was an aristocrat from a pagan family and an ardent disciple of the Neo-Platonist philosopher Hypatia of Alexandria. He has been called the 'Platonist in a Mitre.' Theophilus of Alexandria celebrated the marriage between him and his Christian wife, and subsequently persuaded him to become ever more involved with the Church, eventually pressurizing him to be consecrated bishop. Synesios agreed to this reluctantly. He can just bring himself, he says, to give up his hunting pursuits, but he will not renounce his wife, or his Neo-Platonist speculations. If that is not acceptable, then he should be left alone.

It seems that Theophilus, not otherwise known to be friendly to Platonizers accepted the terms, for Synesios ended his life as Metropolitan of Pentapolis. His Nine Hymns (the 10th is not by him, and is reproduced here as Hymn 31) are a celebration of the supreme deity in a highly Neo-Platonist mode of discourse. Christ is presented in the manner of the divine hero rising through the spheres. The doctrine of the Harrowing of Hell is portrayed in a distinct and vivid manner, depicting Christ as the new Hercules who sends Cerberus cringing back into his lair. Bibliography: cf. Quasten, Vol. 3, pp.106-114, esp. p.113. Text: Lacombrade, pp.94-96.

16. *A song of Christ*, Flavius Merobaudes.

Flavius Merobaudes (*fl.* 435) was a Spanish aristocrat and, after 433, a key member of the circle of Aetius. He rose to high office in the court at Ravenna in the time of Galla Placidia and Valentinian III, becoming *Comes Sacri Consistorii*, a member of the imperial cabinet, bearing a rank equivalent to the Proconsuls of Africa, Asia, and Achaia. He was famous as a soldier-poet in his lifetime, and a bronze statue was dedicated to him in the Roman forum. Its plinth was rediscovered in 1813. The poem *De Christo* is typical of the fine hexameter style of Merobaudes. It was published under the name of Claudian as 'Epigram 98', but it does not belong to him. In the sixteenth century Fabricius first identified Merobaudes as the true author and the ascription is now generally accepted. The terse, driving rhythm of the Latin hexameters urges on his narrative of Christ's redemption in a superbly crafted piece demonstrating no little skill in theology. The text here is taken from *PL* 61, 971-74, ed. Galland. A version can also be found listed under the Claudian *dubia*, though in a more corrupted textual condition, in *PL* 53, 788.

17. *A Lenten Hymn*, Flavius Merobaudes.

This poem in hexameter form is found in the Claudian *dubia* as Epigram 99, *PL* 53, 788-9. It is undoubtedly from the same hand as the poem above, although the Merobaudian authorship has not generally been recognised. Despite its manuscript title of 'Paschal Song' it is clearly a Lenten hymn written in the time of the fasts. It is a highly crafted poetic composition that delights in expressing the paradoxes and contrasts of the redemptive plan. There are some fine touches such as the one who embraces the orb of the world lying now, embraced under the orb of his mother's breast. The strong soteriological drive of the hymn makes it a highly memorable piece.

18. *A Hymn Before Eating*, Aurelius Clemens Prudentius.

Prudentius (*circa* 348-410) is commonly regarded as the greatest of the Latin Christian poets. He was a Spaniard by birth, and a successful lawyer, rising to prominent rank in the civil service of the Empire. In retirement in his fifties he lived in rustic seclusion on his estate, and like many other Roman nobles before him regarded his time of retreat and retirement as an ideal *otium* after the clamour of public life. Prudentius wrote much of his Christian poetry in this period. Both poems representing Prudentius here are taken from his *Cathemerinon*, or 'Hymns For Daily Use.' The original is 205 lines long; here lines 1-20 and 56-65 have been represented. Text: *Cathemerinon* 3, Pope, pp.22-35.

19. *Hymn at the Lighting of the Lamps*, Prudentius.

There is some controversy whether this refers to an Easter Vigil Liturgy, or to the ordinary office of lamplighting. There can be no disagreement, however, that it is an exquisite piece of writing. From a total of 164 lines, this translation represents lines 1-28, and 153-164. Text: *Cathemerinon* 5, Pope, pp.44-57.

20. *A Grace Before Eating*, Byzantine Anonymous.

The hymn is attached to the end of the manuscript of Book 7 of *The Apostolic Constitutions*. Text: Christ-Paranikas, p.40.

21. *A Hymn at Eventide*, Byzantine Anonymous.

The reference to the thrice-holy Saviour perhaps reflects the Trisagion Controversy, where the chant 'Holy God, Holy and Strong, Holy Immortal' was a source of dispute between Monophysites and Chalcedonians as to whether it had a Trinitarian or Christological reference. Text: Trypanis, p.5.

22. *An Evening Hymn*, Byzantine Anonymous.

This hymn, so full of the sense of divine majesty, also seems to have led into the chanting of the Trisagion. Text: Trypanis, pp.4-5.

23. *A Moral Palindrome*, Byzantine Anonymous.

Read either way in Greek it says the same thing. It is a very clever piece of laconic moralizing from a monastic scribe, *circa* 6th century. Text: Trypanis, p.39.

24. *A Christmas Hymn*, St Romanos the Singer.

Romanos was born in Emesa (Homs) in Syria and was deacon in the church at Beirut before coming to Constantinople in the time of Anastasius I. He was attached as choirmaster and priest to the church of the Virgin in the district of Kyrou. His hymns are still sung in the Byzantine liturgy but his style is unlike that of the general run of Byzantine poetry, in so far as it takes a luxuriating delight in word-plays, and strong contrasts. The internal assonances of the Greek stanzas are quite marked, something that cannot be reproduced in English translation. The effect of the whole when set to music is highly original and dynamic. Romanos' main tendency in theology is to set the biblical narrative in a didactic verse commentary. The *Christmas Hymn* is perhaps his most famous composition. Its opening stanzas reveal it as an acrostic which reads down the entire length of the poem as, 'The hymn of the humble Romanos'. The original is twenty-five stanzas in length. Complete works: *Cantica Genuina*, edited by P. Maas and C. Trypanis, Oxford, 1963; *Romanos le Mélode et les origines de la poésie réligieuse à Byzance*, J. Grosdidier de Matons, Paris, 1977. Text here from Trypanis, pp.11, 13.

25. *Hymn on the Resurrection*, St John of Damascus.

John (*circa* 675-749) was an important political leader of the Christian community of Damascus under the Caliphate, holding the office of *Logothete* after his father. He withdrew from the city in the early eighth century, in a climate of increasingly difficult relations with his Islamic overlords. He took refuge in the monastery of Mar Saba, in the Judaean desert near Bethlehem, and was ordained priest there, holding, for a while, the position of priest-in-charge of the Byzantine church on Mount Tabor. From Mar Saba monastery, then outside Byzantine military control, he became a public defender of the icons, in the face of an imperial court that was set on an iconoclastic policy. His Constantinopolitan enemies played on his Syrian family name of Mansur, rendering it into Greek as John 'the Bastard', but his Doctrine of the Images won the day and he was posthumously vindicated at the Seventh Oecumenical Council in 787. He composed numerous hymns, as well as a compendium of theology which represented one of the last great summations of Greek patristic learning. It influenced, in turn, Peter Lombard, and Thomas Aquinas, who used John's theological systematics as a major source for his own *Summa Theologica*. Works in *PG* 94-95. Text here: Christ-Paranikas, p.117.

26. *Hymn to the Virgin*, St John of Damascus.

This *Theotokion* from Evening Prayer uses titles of the Virgin Mary to great effect in demonstrating her role as heavenly intercessor with her Son. The final verse presents the Byzantine sense of being under great threat from Islam in Palestine. In John's day Christian civilisation seemed, especially from the perspective of those who lived on the Eastern borders, to be in constant regression. Text: Christ-Paranikas, pp.117-118.

27. *Hymn to the Life-Giving Cross*, St John of Damascus.

The Crucifixion is presented as Paschal victory that reconstitutes the very nature of mankind in the image of the immortal God. This is something very typical of the Eastern Christian doctrine of redemption. The human race is not only redeemed through the resurrection, but ontologically changed by the gift of deification through grace. Text: Christ-Paranikas, p.118.

28. *Hymn on the Presentation of the Lord*, St John of Damascus.

See the Gospel of Luke 2:22-39. Known in the Western Church as Candlemas, this feast is celebrated on February 2nd. It commemorates Christ's fulfilling of the Jewish law of the redemption of the first-born son by the offering of two turtledoves in the Temple at Jerusalem forty days after his birth. It also commemorates the purification of the Virgin Mary. The feast was kept locally at Jerusalem from about 350.

In 542 the Emperor Justinian ordered its observance at Constantinople as a thanksgiving for the cessation of plague, and it thence spread throughout the East, where it was called 'The Meeting', i.e of Christ with Simeon. Text: Christ-Paranikas, p.120.

29. *A Paschal Song*, Sedulius Scotus.

Sedulius the Irishman (*fl.* 848-74)—not to be confused with the 5th century poet Sedulius—left Ireland as a wandering scholar and travelled to Liége settling there under the patronage of the Archbishop Hartgar. Emperor Lothair I appointed him as tutor to his sons, and during this period he composed a treatise on the art of Christian statesmanship for the young princes Lothair and Charles. He composed numerous poems and scriptural commentaries. While Sedulius was alive he was a veritable centre of Irish culture on the continent. This poem, a fragment from a much larger piece, has never lost its freshness across the span of centuries. The scent of the waxen candles of Easter still hangs with him as he thinks of the bees wandering through fields of poppies. The gathering sound of evensong on Easter Sunday comes to him through the dusk and turns his heart to absent friends. His theological works are found in *PL* 103, 9-352. For the poetic works, see L. Traube, *Monumenta Germaniae Historia*, Vol.3, *Poetae*, 1896, pp.151-240, *Carmina*, 3.2, Lines 17-26.

30. *Hymn to the Virgin Mother of God*, Andrew of Jerusalem, Archbishop of Crete.

Despite his various names, Andrew (*circa* 660-740) was a native of Damascus, finally becoming Archbishop of Gortyna in Crete *circa* 692. He wrote numerous hymns, especially favouring the form of lengthy 'canons', of which poetic form he is said to have been the inventor. His most famous work is the Great Canon (250 strophes) which is used in the Eastern Church's Lenten offices. The present poem in honour of the Virgin Mother of God expresses a fine sense of paradoxes in a laconic restraint of language. His feastday is July 4th. Works in *PG* 97, 805-1444; *The Great Canon* (ET), Derwas Chitty, London, 1957. Text here: Christ-Paranikas, pp.97-8.

31. *The Prayer of the Scribe*, Pseudo Synesios (The Monk George).

This was a copyist's prayer added to the end of Synesios' collection of hymns. The rhythm and style are totally unlike Synesios. While it may not be a masterpiece of literature, it expresses a robust monastic sense of humility, and the essence of the Byzantine ascetic mentality. This poem was the root for the famous translation of Synesios', 'Lord Jesus think on me', in *Hymns Ancient and Modern*. Text: Lacombrade, p.107.

PRIMARY SOURCES

ANET   J. Pritchard, ed., *Ancient Near Eastern Texts Relating to the O.T.* (Princeton, 1955)

PG   J.P. Migne, ed., *Cursus Completus Patrologiae Graecae*, 162 vols. (Paris, 1857-66)

PL   J.P. Migne, ed., *Cursus Completus Patrologiae Latinae*, 221 vols. (Paris, 1844-64)

SELECT BIBLIOGRAPHY

Berardino, A. di, *Patrology*, Vol. 4, 'Christian Poetry', pp.255-341 (Westminster, MD, 1986)

Brownlie, J., *Hymns of The Early Church* (London, 1913)

Cantarella, R., *Poeti Byzantini*, Vols.1-2 (Milan, 1948)

Christ, W., and M. Paranikas, *Anthologia Graeca Carminum Christianorum* (Leipzig, 1871)

Fitzgerald, A., *The Essays and Hymns of Synesius of Cyrene* (Oxford, 1926)

The Great Horologion (Venice, 1856)

Lacombrade, C., *Synesios de Cyrene: Hymnes* (Paris, 1978)

McGuckin, J.A., *St Gregory Nazianzen: Selected Poems* (SLG Press, Oxford, 1986, 1989)

Pope, R.M., *The Hymns of Prudentius* (London, 1905)

Quasten, J., *Patrology*, Vols.1-3 (Utrecht, 1975)

Saliveros, M., *The Divine Liturgy* (Athens, 1924)

Sanders, J.T., *The New Testament Christological Hymns* (Cambridge, 1971)

Trypanis, C.A., *Medieval and Modern Greek Poetry* (Oxford, 1951)

Waddell, H., *Medieval Latin Lyrics* (London, 5th edn, 1975)

Ware, K., and Mother Maria, *The Akathistos Hymn to the Most Holy Mother of God and Office of Small Compline* (Ecumenical Society of the Blessed Virgin Mary, Wallington, 1987)

Wellesz, E., *A History of Byzantine Music and Hymnography* (Oxford, 1949)